# Table of Contents

# Chapter 1: Understanding Scrum

## 1.1. The Genesis of Scrum

Scrum, in the realm of project management and software development, stands as a dynamic and adaptive framework that has revolutionized the way teams collaborate, innovate, and deliver value to stakeholders. Its genesis can be traced back to the early 1980s when Hirotaka Takeuchi and Ikujiro Nonaka, two Japanese professors, published a seminal paper titled "The New New Product Development Game" in the Harvard Business Review. This paper introduced the concept of Scrum as a response to the traditional, rigid approaches that were prevalent at the time.

In their paper, Takeuchi and Nonaka drew inspiration from the game of rugby, where a team works together in a complex, unpredictable environment to achieve a common goal. They observed that successful product development shared similarities with the rugby game, and thus, the term "Scrum" was coined. Scrum, in this context, referred to the tight-knit collaboration, adaptability, and relentless pursuit of goals that rugby teams exhibited.

The core idea behind Scrum was to create a framework that could adapt to the rapidly changing demands of the business world and foster innovation. This marked a departure from traditional, plan-driven methodologies that often led to delays and mismatches with evolving customer needs.

### Principles of Scrum

At its heart, Scrum is built upon a set of core principles that guide its implementation:

1. **Transparency:** Scrum emphasizes transparency in all aspects of work. Team members, stakeholders, and customers should have a clear view of progress, challenges, and objectives.

2. **Inspection:** Frequent inspection of work and progress is vital to ensure that the project stays on track. This inspection allows for early identification and resolution of issues.

3. **Adaptation:** Scrum promotes adaptability. Teams are encouraged to adapt to changing circumstances, requirements, and feedback, enabling them to deliver valuable results even in uncertain environments.

These principles provide a solid foundation for Scrum and are woven into the fabric of the framework. They guide the roles, events, and artifacts that make up Scrum, ensuring that the framework remains true to its agile and innovative roots.

### Evolution of Scrum

Since its inception, Scrum has evolved significantly. It was further refined by Ken Schwaber and Jeff Sutherland in the early 1990s, who collaborated to create the Scrum Guide, a comprehensive reference for implementing Scrum. This guide established a common language and framework for Scrum teams and organizations.

Over the years, Scrum has gained widespread adoption not only in software development but also in various other industries. Its adaptability and focus on delivering value have made it a valuable asset in domains as diverse as marketing, manufacturing, education, and more.

In the chapters that follow, we will delve deeper into the principles, roles, events, and artifacts that constitute the Scrum framework. We will explore how Scrum has transformed project management and how it can be applied to different contexts, making it a versatile and powerful approach to work.

---

## 1.2. Core Principles of Scrum Methodology

The Scrum methodology is underpinned by a set of core principles that guide its implementation and foster an agile and collaborative work environment. These principles are the building blocks of Scrum, and understanding them is essential for successful adoption. In this section, we will explore these core principles in detail.

### 1. Empirical Process Control

Scrum is rooted in the idea of empirical process control, which means that decisions are made based on observations and experiences rather than on predefined plans. This principle recognizes that in complex and unpredictable environments, such as software development, it is impossible to anticipate and plan for every detail. Instead, Scrum encourages teams to continuously inspect and adapt their work based on real-world feedback.

### 2. Iterative and Incremental Development

Scrum promotes an iterative and incremental approach to development. Rather than attempting to deliver a complete product at the end of a long development cycle, Scrum teams work in short, time-boxed iterations called "Sprints." Each Sprint typically lasts two to four weeks and results in a potentially shippable product increment. This incremental delivery allows for early feedback and ensures that valuable features are prioritized and delivered sooner.

### 3. Self-Organizing Teams

Scrum relies on self-organizing teams that have the autonomy to make decisions about how they will achieve their Sprint goals. This autonomy empowers team members to take ownership of their work and collaborate effectively. The Scrum Master's role is to coach and facilitate, rather than to micromanage the team.

## 4. Cross-Functional Teams

Scrum teams are composed of individuals with diverse skills and expertise, often referred to as cross-functional teams. This diversity ensures that the team has all the necessary skills to deliver a complete product increment. Cross-functional teams are more adaptable and can tackle a wide range of challenges, leading to higher efficiency and better outcomes.

## 5. Time-Boxed Events

Scrum introduces a set of time-boxed events, including Sprint Planning, Daily Stand-ups, Sprint Review, and Sprint Retrospective. These events provide structure to the Scrum framework and enable regular inspection and adaptation. Time-boxing ensures that meetings remain focused and efficient, preventing them from becoming time-consuming and unproductive.

## 6. Collaboration and Transparency

Collaboration and transparency are fundamental to Scrum's success. Scrum teams collaborate closely with stakeholders, including Product Owners and customers, to ensure that the product meets their needs. Transparency is achieved through open and honest communication, making work and progress visible to all stakeholders.

## 7. Delivering Value

Scrum places a strong emphasis on delivering value to customers and stakeholders. It prioritizes work based on its value and ensures that valuable features are delivered early and frequently. This focus on value drives customer satisfaction and helps organizations remain competitive in the market.

## 8. Continuous Improvement

Continuous improvement is at the heart of Scrum. Teams regularly inspect their processes and seek opportunities to improve. The Sprint Retrospective event, in particular, is dedicated to reflecting on what went well and what could be improved. This commitment to continuous improvement allows Scrum teams to adapt and excel over time.

By embracing these core principles, Scrum provides a framework that enables organizations to navigate the complexities of modern project management and deliver value in an agile and responsive manner. In the following chapters, we will explore how these principles are applied in practice and how Scrum teams effectively implement them to achieve their goals.

## 1.3. Roles in Scrum: An Overview

Roles are a fundamental component of the Scrum framework, and they play distinct and crucial roles in ensuring the success of Scrum projects. In this section, we will provide an overview of the key roles in Scrum, each with its unique responsibilities and contributions.

### 1.3.1. Product Owner

The Product Owner is a central figure in Scrum and holds the responsibility for maximizing the value delivered by the Scrum team. Their primary duties include:

- **Product Vision:** The Product Owner defines and communicates a clear product vision, ensuring that the team understands the long-term goals and objectives.

- **Backlog Management:** They are responsible for creating and maintaining the Product Backlog, a prioritized list of features, enhancements, and user stories that represent the product's requirements.

- **Prioritization:** The Product Owner determines the priority of items in the Product Backlog based on business value and stakeholder needs.

- **Acceptance Criteria:** They define acceptance criteria for each item in the Product Backlog, ensuring that the team understands what constitutes a complete and satisfactory implementation.

- **Collaboration:** Product Owners collaborate closely with the development team, Scrum Master, and stakeholders to ensure that the product is developed in line with business objectives and customer requirements.

### 1.3.2. Scrum Master

The Scrum Master is a servant-leader who facilitates and coaches the Scrum team and ensures that Scrum principles and practices are followed. Their key responsibilities include:

- **Scrum Guidance:** The Scrum Master guides the team in understanding and implementing Scrum principles, practices, and values.

- **Obstacle Removal:** They identify and remove impediments and obstacles that hinder the team's progress, enabling a smooth workflow.

- **Facilitation:** Scrum Masters facilitate Scrum events such as Sprint Planning, Daily Stand-ups, Sprint Review, and Sprint Retrospective, ensuring they are effective and productive.

- **Continuous Improvement:** They promote a culture of continuous improvement within the team, helping them identify and address areas for growth.

- **Servant Leadership:** Scrum Masters serve the team by coaching, mentoring, and facilitating, but they do not dictate how the team should work or make decisions for them.



The Development Team is a self-organizing and cross-functional group responsible for delivering a potentially shippable product increment at the end of each Sprint. Key aspects of the Development Team include:

- **Self-Organization:** The team has the autonomy to decide how to best achieve the Sprint goal and how to organize their work.

- **Cross-Functionality:** It consists of individuals with diverse skills, including developers, testers, designers, and other roles needed to deliver a complete product.

- **Sprint Commitment:** The team commits to delivering a set of product backlog items during the Sprint and works collaboratively to achieve that commitment.

- **Continuous Delivery:** The Development Team focuses on delivering a potentially shippable product increment at the end of each Sprint, with a goal of achieving this in every Sprint.



Stakeholders are individuals or groups outside the Scrum team who have an interest in the product being developed. They may include customers, users, executives, and others. Key points about stakeholders are:

- **Feedback and Collaboration:** Stakeholders provide feedback, review product increments, and collaborate with the Scrum team to ensure that the product aligns with their needs and expectations.

- **Product Vision:** They should align with the Product Owner's vision for the product and work together to prioritize and refine the Product Backlog.

- **Transparency:** Scrum encourages transparency, and stakeholders have visibility into the progress and status of the project.

These are the core roles in Scrum, and each has a vital role in the successful delivery of valuable products. Understanding the responsibilities and interactions among these roles is essential for implementing Scrum effectively. In the subsequent chapters, we will explore each role in more detail and delve into their specific responsibilities and challenges.

## 1.4. The Scrum Framework: A Bird's Eye View

The Scrum framework provides a structured approach to Agile project management, emphasizing collaboration, adaptability, and value delivery. At its core, Scrum consists of defined roles, events, and artifacts that work together to guide the development process. In this section, we'll take a bird's eye view of the Scrum framework, providing an overview of its components.

### 1.4.1. Scrum Roles

Scrum defines three primary roles, each with distinct responsibilities:

- **Product Owner:** The Product Owner represents the customer or stakeholder and is responsible for defining and prioritizing the product backlog.

- **Scrum Master:** The Scrum Master is a servant-leader who facilitates the Scrum process, removes impediments, and ensures the team adheres to Scrum principles.

- **Development Team:** A self-organizing, cross-functional group responsible for delivering a potentially shippable product increment at the end of each sprint.

### 1.4.2. Scrum Events

Scrum events are time-boxed meetings and ceremonies that provide structure to the Scrum framework:

- **Sprint:** A time-boxed iteration, typically lasting 2-4 weeks, during which a potentially shippable product increment is developed.

- **Sprint Planning:** The team collaboratively plans the work for the upcoming sprint, selecting items from the product backlog.

- **Daily Stand-up:** A brief daily meeting where team members share progress, discuss impediments, and plan for the day.

- **Sprint Review:** A meeting at the end of the sprint where the team presents the product increment to stakeholders for feedback.

- **Sprint Retrospective:** A reflective meeting at the end of the sprint where the team discusses what went well, what could be improved, and creates action items for the next sprint.

### 1.4.3. Scrum Artifacts

Scrum artifacts are information radiators that provide transparency and information about the project:

- **Product Backlog:** A prioritized list of features, enhancements, and user stories that represent the product's requirements.

- **Sprint Backlog:** A subset of the product backlog items selected for the current sprint and a plan for how to achieve them.

- **Potentially Shippable Product Increment:** The result of a sprint, consisting of completed product backlog items and potentially ready for release.

### 1.4.4. Scrum Flow

The Scrum framework follows a structured flow that involves continuous iterations:

1. **Product Backlog Refinement:** The Product Owner continually refines and prioritizes the product backlog.

2. **Sprint Planning:** The team plans the work for the upcoming sprint, selecting items from the product backlog and creating a sprint backlog.

3. **Sprint:** The team works on the sprint backlog, focusing on delivering a potentially shippable product increment.

4. **Daily Stand-up:** Daily meetings keep the team aligned, and any impediments are addressed.

5. **Sprint Review:** The team presents the product increment to stakeholders for feedback.

6. **Sprint Retrospective:** The team reflects on the sprint and identifies areas for improvement.

7. **Start a New Sprint:** The cycle repeats with a new sprint, incorporating feedback and lessons learned.

### 1.4.5. Scrum Values

Scrum is guided by five core values:

- **Commitment:** Team members are committed to achieving sprint goals and delivering value.

- **Courage:** Team members have the courage to speak up, make tough decisions, and confront challenges.

- **Focus:** The team maintains a laser focus on achieving sprint goals and delivering a potentially shippable product increment.

- **Openness:** Transparency and open communication are encouraged within the team and with stakeholders.

- **Respect:** Team members respect each other's perspectives, skills, and contributions.

Understanding this bird's eye view of the Scrum framework is essential before diving into the details of each component. Scrum's structure and values provide a solid foundation for Agile project management and can be adapted to various industries and project types. In the following chapters, we will explore each aspect of Scrum in greater detail to provide a comprehensive understanding of this powerful framework.

## 1.5. Scrum vs. Traditional Project Management

Scrum, as an Agile framework, stands in contrast to traditional project management methodologies, which often follow a more linear and predictive approach. In this section, we will compare and contrast Scrum with traditional project management, highlighting the key differences and the advantages Scrum offers in today's dynamic business environment.

### 1.5.1. Approach to Planning

*Traditional Project Management:*

In traditional project management, planning is typically done upfront in detail, with a comprehensive project plan created at the beginning of the project. This plan outlines all the project requirements, tasks, timelines, and resources. Any changes to the plan require formal change control procedures, which can be time-consuming and bureaucratic.

*Scrum:*

Scrum takes an adaptive approach to planning. While there is some initial planning, the focus is on short-term planning within each sprint. The product backlog is prioritized, and the team selects items for the upcoming sprint during sprint planning. This flexibility allows for adapting to changing requirements and priorities more effectively.

### 1.5.2. Change Management

*Traditional Project Management:*

In traditional project management, changes to project requirements or scope are often met with resistance. Formal change requests need to be processed, and changes can lead to project delays and increased costs.

*Scrum:*

Scrum embraces change. Changes can be easily accommodated at the beginning of each sprint or even mid-sprint. The product backlog is dynamic, and the team can reprioritize and adjust their work based on new information or stakeholder feedback.

### 1.5.3. Project Control

*Traditional Project Management:*

Traditional project management relies on strict control mechanisms to ensure that the project stays on track. Detailed plans and regular status reports are used to monitor progress and deviations from the plan.

*Scrum:*

Scrum relies on transparency and inspection rather than control. Progress is visible through artifacts like the product backlog, sprint backlog, and burndown charts. Instead of rigid control, Scrum promotes self-organization and trust in the development team.

### 1.5.4. Flexibility and Adaptability

*Traditional Project Management:*

Traditional methodologies are often less flexible and struggle to adapt to changing requirements or market conditions. Changes may require significant paperwork and approval processes.

*Scrum:*

Scrum is highly adaptable. It encourages frequent inspection and adaptation, allowing teams to respond quickly to changes. This adaptability is especially valuable in industries with rapidly changing markets or technologies.

### 1.5.5. Stakeholder Engagement

*Traditional Project Management:*

Stakeholder engagement is often limited to predefined project phases, such as requirements gathering and project delivery. Stakeholders may have limited visibility into the project's progress until it's near completion.

*Scrum:*

Scrum emphasizes continuous stakeholder engagement. Stakeholders are involved throughout the project, providing feedback during sprint reviews and having access to the product incrementally. This ensures that the product aligns with their expectations and needs.

### 1.5.6. Risk Management

*Traditional Project Management:*

Risk management in traditional methodologies often involves identifying risks upfront and developing mitigation plans. However, it may not address emerging risks effectively.

Scrum embraces a more proactive approach to risk management. Risks can be identified and addressed throughout the project, with the ability to adapt and pivot as needed.

### 1.5.7. Delivery Frequency

*Traditional Project Management:*

In traditional project management, the final product is typically delivered at the end of the project, which can be a lengthy period.

*Scrum:*

Scrum focuses on delivering a potentially shippable product increment at the end of each sprint. This frequent delivery allows for faster feedback and the opportunity to release valuable features sooner.

In conclusion, while traditional project management methodologies have their place, Scrum offers a more agile and adaptive approach that aligns with the demands of today's fast-paced business landscape. Scrum's emphasis on collaboration, flexibility, and delivering value iteratively has made it a popular choice for organizations seeking to stay competitive and responsive to changing customer needs. Understanding the differences between Scrum and traditional project management is crucial for making informed decisions about which approach best suits a given project or organization.

# Chapter 2: The Role of the Scrum Master

## 2.1. Who is a Scrum Master?

The role of a Scrum Master is central to the success of Scrum teams and projects. In this section, we will delve into what a Scrum Master is, their core responsibilities, and the qualities that make a Scrum Master effective.

### 2.1.1. Definition of a Scrum Master

A Scrum Master is a servant-leader who acts as a coach, facilitator, and mentor to a Scrum team. They are responsible for ensuring that the team follows Scrum practices, values, and principles, ultimately helping the team to deliver high-quality products. The Scrum Master serves as a bridge between the team and external stakeholders, ensuring that communication flows smoothly and that impediments are removed.

### 2.1.2. Key Responsibilities of a Scrum Master

*1. **Coaching and Mentoring:** The Scrum Master coaches the team on Scrum practices and principles. They help team members understand their roles, responsibilities, and the Scrum framework itself. Additionally, they mentor the team on self-organization and continuous improvement.*

*2. **Facilitation:** Scrum Masters facilitate Scrum events, including Sprint Planning, Daily Stand-ups, Sprint Review, and Sprint Retrospective. They ensure that these meetings run effectively and help the team stay focused on their goals.*

*3. **Removing Impediments:** A significant part of a Scrum Master's role is identifying and removing impediments that hinder the team's progress. Whether it's dealing with organizational obstacles or team-specific issues, the Scrum Master works to create a smoother path for the team.*

*4. **Promoting Self-Organization:** Scrum Masters foster a self-organizing team culture. They encourage team members to take ownership of their work, make decisions collectively, and continuously improve their processes.*

*5. **Protecting the Team:** Scrum Masters shield the team from external disruptions and excessive demands. They ensure that the team can focus on their work during the sprint and have the time and space to deliver the best possible results.*

*6. **Continuous Learning:** Scrum Masters are lifelong learners. They stay up-to-date with Scrum best practices, Agile methodologies, and industry trends. This knowledge helps them guide the team effectively.*

*7. **Facilitating Collaboration:** Scrum Masters promote collaboration between team members, the Product Owner, and stakeholders. They ensure that everyone involved in the project works together toward common goals.*

*8. **Monitoring Progress:** While not responsible for managing the team's work, Scrum Masters monitor progress using tools like burndown charts or task boards. This helps them identify areas where the team might need support or improvement.*

### 2.1.3. Qualities of an Effective Scrum Master

Being an effective Scrum Master requires a unique set of qualities and characteristics:

- **Empathy:** An effective Scrum Master is empathetic and understands the team's challenges and concerns. They are supportive and strive to create a safe and inclusive environment.

- **Servant Leadership:** Scrum Masters practice servant leadership, putting the team's needs first and facilitating their success.

- **Communication Skills:** Strong communication skills are essential. Scrum Masters must convey information clearly and facilitate effective communication within the team and with stakeholders.

- **Adaptability:** Scrum Masters adapt to changing circumstances, helping the team navigate uncertainty and complexity.

- **Conflict Resolution:** They have the ability to resolve conflicts within the team and mediate disagreements, promoting harmony and collaboration.

- **Continuous Improvement:** An effective Scrum Master is committed to their own growth and the growth of the team. They seek opportunities for improvement and are open to feedback.

- **Problem Solving:** They are skilled problem solvers, able to identify issues and work collaboratively to find solutions.

- **Organizational Awareness:** Scrum Masters understand the organization's culture, processes, and dynamics, which helps them navigate and advocate for the team within the organization.

- **Courage:** They have the courage to speak up, challenge the status quo, and protect the team from external pressures that could compromise their productivity or quality.

In summary, a Scrum Master plays a pivotal role in guiding and supporting Scrum teams on their Agile journey. They possess a unique combination of skills, qualities, and responsibilities that enable them to serve the team and promote the successful implementation of Scrum practices. Understanding the essence of a Scrum Master is crucial for anyone aspiring to excel in this role or work effectively with one.

## 2.2. Key Responsibilities of a Scrum Master

The role of a Scrum Master encompasses a wide range of responsibilities that are crucial to the success of a Scrum team and the effective implementation of the Scrum framework. In this section, we will delve into the key responsibilities of a Scrum Master in more detail.

### 2.2.1. Coaching and Mentoring

Coaching and mentoring are at the core of a Scrum Master's role. They guide and support the Scrum team in understanding and embracing Scrum principles and practices. This includes helping team members learn about their roles, the Scrum framework, and Agile principles. Through coaching and mentoring, a Scrum Master empowers the team to self-organize, make decisions, and continuously improve.

Scrum Masters play a pivotal role in facilitating Scrum events, which are essential for transparency, inspection, and adaptation. These events include:

- **Sprint Planning:** The Scrum Master helps the team plan the work for the upcoming Sprint, ensuring that the team selects the right items from the Product Backlog and understands the Sprint goal.

- **Daily Stand-up:** They facilitate the Daily Stand-up meeting where team members share progress, discuss impediments, and plan their activities for the day. The Scrum Master ensures the meeting remains focused and time-bound.

- **Sprint Review:** Scrum Masters facilitate the Sprint Review, where the team presents the product increment to stakeholders and collects feedback. This event helps in understanding the product's progress and aligning it with stakeholder expectations.

- **Sprint Retrospective:** The Scrum Master guides the team in conducting a Sprint Retrospective, where they reflect on their processes, identify improvement opportunities, and create action items for the next Sprint. This retrospective process promotes continuous improvement.

## 2.2.3. Removing Impediments

One of the most critical responsibilities of a Scrum Master is identifying and removing impediments that hinder the team's progress. Impediments can come from various sources, including organizational issues, resource constraints, or conflicts within the team. The Scrum Master acts as a problem solver and advocate for the team, ensuring that impediments are addressed promptly to maintain the team's productivity.

## 2.2.4. Protecting the Team

Scrum Masters protect the Scrum team from external disruptions and excessive demands. They create a shield that allows the team to focus on their work during the Sprint. By managing distractions and shielding the team from unnecessary pressure, the Scrum Master helps create an environment where the team can thrive and deliver high-quality work.

## 2.2.5. Promoting Self-Organization

Scrum Masters foster a culture of self-organization within the team. They encourage team members to take ownership of their work, make decisions collectively, and continuously improve their processes. This autonomy empowers the team to make informed choices and adapt to changing circumstances, which is fundamental to the Agile mindset.

## 2.2.6. Continuous Learning

Scrum Masters are lifelong learners who stay updated with Scrum best practices, Agile methodologies, and industry trends. Their continuous learning helps them provide valuable guidance to the team and navigate evolving challenges effectively. Being well-informed allows them to adapt and incorporate new ideas and approaches into the Scrum framework.

### 2.2.7. Facilitating Collaboration

Collaboration is a cornerstone of Scrum, and Scrum Masters play a key role in facilitating collaboration between team members, the Product Owner, and stakeholders. They ensure that everyone involved in the project works together toward common goals and that communication flows smoothly. Effective collaboration leads to better understanding, alignment, and ultimately, the delivery of value.

### 2.2.8. Monitoring Progress

While Scrum Masters are not responsible for managing the team's work, they monitor progress using tools like burndown charts, task boards, or other metrics relevant to the project. This monitoring helps them identify areas where the team might need support or improvement. By keeping an eye on progress, Scrum Masters can provide valuable insights and guidance to the team.

In summary, the responsibilities of a Scrum Master are multifaceted and encompass various aspects of coaching, facilitating, problem-solving, and advocacy. A skilled Scrum Master plays a pivotal role in helping the Scrum team navigate challenges, embrace Agile principles, and continuously improve their processes. Understanding and fulfilling these key responsibilities are essential for effectively serving as a Scrum Master and supporting the team's success.

## 2.3. The Scrum Master's Toolbox: Essential Skills and Abilities

To be an effective Scrum Master, one needs a diverse set of skills and abilities that go beyond understanding Scrum practices. In this section, we will explore the toolbox of essential skills and qualities that enable Scrum Masters to excel in their role.

### 2.3.1. Strong Communication Skills

Effective communication is at the heart of a Scrum Master's role. Scrum Masters must be able to convey information clearly, facilitate discussions, and ensure that all team members, stakeholders, and the Product Owner are on the same page. They should be active listeners who can understand and empathize with others' perspectives and concerns.

### 2.3.2. Empathy

Empathy is the ability to understand and share the feelings of others. Scrum Masters need to be empathetic to build strong relationships within the team and with stakeholders. By understanding the team's challenges and concerns, Scrum Masters can provide support and create a safe and inclusive environment where team members feel valued.

### 2.3.3. Servant Leadership

Servant leadership is a leadership philosophy that emphasizes serving others first. Scrum Masters practice servant leadership by putting the needs of the team before their own. They empower the team to make decisions, encourage self-organization, and focus on the team's growth and success.

### 2.3.4. Conflict Resolution Skills

Conflict is a natural part of any team, and Scrum Masters should be skilled in resolving conflicts effectively. They mediate disagreements within the team, facilitate open and respectful communication, and help team members find common ground. Resolving conflicts promotes a healthy team dynamic.

### 2.3.5. Problem-Solving Abilities

Scrum Masters should be adept problem solvers. They need to identify impediments and challenges that hinder the team's progress and work collaboratively to find solutions. Problem-solving involves a combination of critical thinking, creativity, and resourcefulness.

### 2.3.6. Adaptability

Adaptability is crucial in the ever-changing landscape of Agile projects. Scrum Masters should be able to adapt to evolving circumstances, requirements, and priorities. They need to guide the team through uncertainty and help them pivot when necessary.

### 2.3.7. Courage

Courage is the willingness to speak up, make tough decisions, and confront challenges. Scrum Masters need the courage to address issues within the team or with stakeholders. They should be advocates for the team's well-being and be unafraid to challenge the status quo when it hinders progress.

### 2.3.8. Time Management

Time management skills are essential for Scrum Masters to ensure that Scrum events, such as Sprint Planning, Daily Stand-ups, and Retrospectives, run efficiently and stay within their time boxes. Effective time management helps keep the team focused and productive.

### 2.3.9. Facilitation Skills

Scrum Masters often serve as facilitators during Scrum events and meetings. They should have strong facilitation skills to guide discussions, keep meetings on track, and encourage active participation from all team members.

### 2.3.10. Technical Knowledge (Optional)

While not mandatory, having technical knowledge relevant to the project can be advantageous for a Scrum Master. It can help them understand the team's work better and provide more meaningful support. However, technical expertise should not overshadow the Scrum Master's primary responsibilities, which focus on facilitating the Scrum process and team dynamics.

### 2.3.11. Organizational Awareness

Scrum Masters should have a good understanding of the organization's culture, processes, and dynamics. This awareness enables them to navigate the organization effectively, advocate for the team, and identify potential challenges or opportunities for improvement.

### 2.3.12. Continuous Learning

Scrum is an ever-evolving field, and Scrum Masters should be committed to continuous learning. Staying up-to-date with Scrum best practices, Agile methodologies, and industry trends equips them with the knowledge needed to guide the team effectively.

### 2.3.13. Resilience

Resilience is the ability to bounce back from setbacks and maintain a positive attitude during challenging times. Scrum Masters should be resilient, as they may encounter obstacles and setbacks in their role. Maintaining a constructive and optimistic outlook helps them support the team through difficulties.

### 2.3.14. Data-Driven Decision-Making

Scrum Masters can benefit from the ability to make data-driven decisions. They should be familiar with Agile metrics and use them to monitor progress, identify areas for improvement, and make informed decisions to enhance the team's performance.

In summary, the Scrum Master's toolbox is diverse and multifaceted, encompassing a wide range of skills, qualities, and abilities. These attributes, along with a deep understanding of Scrum principles, enable Scrum Masters to excel in their role as servant-leaders, coaches, and facilitators of Agile teams. Mastering these skills and continuously improving them is essential for a Scrum Master to navigate the challenges of Agile project management successfully.

---

## 2.4. Scrum Master as a Servant Leader

The concept of servant leadership is at the core of the Scrum Master's role. In this section, we will explore what it means for a Scrum Master to be a servant leader and how this approach benefits Scrum teams.

Servant leadership is a leadership philosophy that prioritizes serving others before oneself. It was coined by Robert K. Greenleaf in the 1970s and has since gained recognition as an effective leadership approach in Agile and Scrum contexts.

At its essence, a servant leader is someone who:

- **Puts the needs of others first:** A servant leader focuses on the well-being and growth of their team members. They prioritize the team's success and individual development.

- **Listens actively:** Servant leaders are active listeners who seek to understand others' perspectives, concerns, and aspirations. They create an environment where team members feel heard and valued.

- **Empowers and supports:** Servant leaders empower their teams by providing the autonomy to make decisions, take ownership, and self-organize. They offer guidance and support when needed.

- **Facilitates collaboration:** Servant leaders promote collaboration within the team and across stakeholders. They encourage open communication and foster a culture of trust and cooperation.



In the context of Scrum, a Scrum Master embodies the principles of servant leadership:

- **Putting the team first:** The Scrum Master's primary responsibility is to serve the Scrum team. They ensure that the team has the resources, information, and support needed to succeed. The team's goals and well-being are their top priorities.

- **Active listening:** Scrum Masters actively listen to the team's concerns, challenges, and ideas. They facilitate open communication within the team and with stakeholders, creating an environment where everyone's voice is heard.

- **Empowering the team:** Servant leaders empower their teams to self-organize and make decisions. Scrum Masters encourage the team to take ownership of their work, plan their Sprints, and continuously improve their processes.

- **Removing impediments:** A crucial aspect of servant leadership is identifying and removing impediments that hinder the team's progress. Scrum Masters act as advocates for the team, addressing issues and ensuring that the team can work effectively.

- **Facilitating collaboration:** Scrum Masters facilitate collaboration between team members, the Product Owner, and stakeholders. They create a space where all parties can work together toward common goals and make informed decisions.

Embracing servant leadership in the Scrum Master role brings several benefits to Scrum teams and organizations:

- **Improved team morale:** When team members feel supported, heard, and empowered, their morale and job satisfaction increase. This positive environment leads to higher productivity and engagement.

- **Increased team autonomy:** Servant leaders trust their teams to make decisions and self-organize. This autonomy fosters a sense of ownership and responsibility, driving better results.

- **Enhanced problem-solving:** Active listening and open communication allow servant leaders to better understand challenges and find collaborative solutions. This results in more effective problem-solving within the team.

- **Faster issue resolution:** Scrum Masters who act as servant leaders can quickly identify and address impediments, ensuring that the team's progress remains unhampered. This leads to smoother and more predictable Sprint outcomes.

- **Stronger collaboration:** By facilitating collaboration and trust, servant leaders create an environment where teamwork thrives. This collaborative spirit extends beyond the Scrum team, benefiting the entire organization.

- **Sustainable improvement:** Servant leaders focus on continuous improvement, both for the team and themselves. This commitment to growth leads to ongoing enhancements in team performance and Agile practices.

In summary, the Scrum Master's role as a servant leader is fundamental to the success of Scrum teams. By prioritizing the team's needs, active listening, empowering team members, and facilitating collaboration, Scrum Masters create an environment where Agile values and principles can flourish. This approach not only benefits the team but also contributes to the overall success and agility of the organization.

---

## 2.5. The Scrum Master and Team Dynamics

The Scrum Master plays a vital role in shaping and optimizing the dynamics of a Scrum team. In this section, we will explore how the Scrum Master contributes to building and maintaining healthy team dynamics, which are crucial for the success of Agile projects.

### 2.5.1. Team Formation and Development

Team dynamics evolve through various stages of team formation and development. The Scrum Master is instrumental in guiding the team through these phases:

- **Forming:** In the initial stage, team members are often getting to know each other, and roles and responsibilities may not be clear. The Scrum Master helps set expectations, introduces Scrum principles, and facilitates team introductions to establish trust and open communication.

- **Storming:** As the team begins working together, conflicts and disagreements can arise. The Scrum Master assists in addressing conflicts constructively, mediating disputes, and ensuring that team members learn to collaborate effectively.

- **Norming:** In this stage, the team starts to establish norms and processes that work for them. The Scrum Master supports the team in defining their working agreements and adapting Scrum practices to their needs.

- **Performing:** At the performing stage, the team is functioning at its highest potential, delivering value consistently. The Scrum Master continues to foster an environment of continuous improvement and supports the team in sustaining its performance.

## 2.5.2. Facilitating Communication

Effective communication is a cornerstone of healthy team dynamics. The Scrum Master ensures that communication flows smoothly within the team, with the Product Owner, and with stakeholders:

- **Daily Stand-ups:** The Scrum Master facilitates Daily Stand-up meetings to ensure that team members share progress, challenges, and plans. They encourage concise updates and address any impediments raised during the meeting.

- **Sprint Review:** During the Sprint Review, the Scrum Master helps the team present their work to stakeholders and collects feedback. They ensure that feedback is constructive and that it aligns with the Sprint goal.

- **Sprint Retrospective:** The Scrum Master guides the team in conducting effective Sprint Retrospectives. They encourage team members to reflect on their processes, identify improvement opportunities, and create action items for the next Sprint.

- **Stakeholder Engagement:** Scrum Masters promote continuous collaboration with stakeholders, ensuring that their feedback and needs are considered throughout the project. They act as a bridge between the team and stakeholders, facilitating communication and transparency.

## 2.5.3. Conflict Resolution

Conflict is a natural part of team dynamics, and the Scrum Master plays a pivotal role in resolving conflicts promptly and constructively. They use their conflict resolution skills to mediate disagreements, encourage open dialogue, and guide the team toward consensus.

### 2.5.4. Coaching and Mentoring

Coaching and mentoring are ongoing activities for a Scrum Master. They coach team members on Agile principles and practices, provide guidance on Scrum roles and responsibilities, and mentor individuals on personal and professional growth. This coaching helps team members improve their skills and adapt to the Agile mindset.

### 2.5.5. Continuous Improvement

A fundamental aspect of team dynamics is a commitment to continuous improvement. The Scrum Master fosters a culture of continuous improvement within the team by:

- **Encouraging Retrospectives:** The Scrum Master ensures that the team conducts regular Sprint Retrospectives to reflect on their processes and identify areas for improvement.

- **Implementing Feedback:** Feedback collected during Sprint Reviews and from stakeholders is used to drive improvements in the product and processes.

- **Facilitating Experimentation:** Scrum Masters encourage the team to experiment with new approaches, tools, and practices to discover what works best for them.

- **Monitoring Metrics:** They use Agile metrics and data to track progress and identify opportunities for optimization.

### 2.5.6. Promoting Psychological Safety

Psychological safety is crucial for team members to feel comfortable sharing ideas, taking risks, and admitting mistakes. The Scrum Master creates an environment where team members feel safe and supported, which leads to increased creativity, innovation, and collaboration.

### 2.5.7. Shielding the Team

Scrum Masters shield the team from external disruptions and unnecessary pressure, allowing the team to focus on their work. They protect the team's time and ensure that they can deliver value without undue stress.

In summary, the Scrum Master's role in team dynamics is multifaceted and crucial to creating a productive, collaborative, and continuously improving environment. By guiding the team through its stages of development, facilitating effective communication, resolving conflicts, and promoting a culture of continuous improvement, Scrum Masters contribute significantly to the success of Agile projects and the well-being of the team members.

# Chapter 3: Setting the Stage for Scrum

## 3.1. Creating an Agile Environment

Creating an Agile environment is a foundational step in implementing Scrum successfully. It involves setting the stage for Agile principles and practices to thrive within your organization. In this section, we will explore the key elements of creating an Agile environment.

### 3.1.1. Leadership Support

Agile transformation begins at the top. Leadership support is essential for creating an Agile environment. Executives and managers should understand the benefits of Agile methodologies and champion the change. They need to align their goals with Agile principles and actively support Agile initiatives.

### 3.1.2. Agile Mindset

Adopting an Agile mindset is fundamental. Team members at all levels should embrace the Agile values and principles outlined in the Agile Manifesto. This includes valuing individuals and interactions over processes and tools, working collaboratively with customers, responding to change, and delivering value iteratively.

### 3.1.3. Agile Training and Education

Education is key to building an Agile environment. Team members, including managers and stakeholders, should receive proper training in Agile methodologies like Scrum. This ensures that everyone understands their roles and responsibilities within the Agile framework.

### 3.1.4. Empowered Teams

In an Agile environment, teams are empowered to make decisions and self-organize. The organization should trust teams to manage their work, plan Sprints, and continuously improve. This empowerment fosters ownership, accountability, and innovation.

### 3.1.5. Cross-Functional Teams

Cross-functional teams bring together individuals with diverse skills and expertise to deliver end-to-end value. Agile environments promote the formation of such teams to increase collaboration and reduce dependencies on external groups.

### 3.1.6. Agile Tools and Infrastructure

Providing the right tools and infrastructure is crucial. Agile teams need tools for project management, communication, and collaboration. Additionally, infrastructure should support automation, continuous integration, and continuous delivery (CI/CD) to streamline the development process.

### 3.1.7. Agile Metrics and Measurement

Agile environments rely on metrics to monitor progress and make data-driven decisions. Organizations should define relevant metrics and measurement practices to assess the health of Agile projects and identify areas for improvement.

### 3.1.8. Agile Workspaces

Physical and virtual workspaces should be designed to facilitate Agile collaboration. Open and flexible work environments encourage communication, while digital tools enable remote collaboration for distributed teams.

### 3.1.9. Agile Rituals and Ceremonies

Agile rituals, such as Daily Stand-ups, Sprint Planning, Sprint Review, and Sprint Retrospectives, should be established and followed consistently. These ceremonies ensure transparency, inspection, and adaptation throughout the project.

### 3.1.10. Agile Governance

Agile governance frameworks should be in place to ensure compliance with organizational policies and regulations while allowing Agile teams the flexibility to work efficiently.

### 3.1.11. Agile Culture

Creating an Agile culture is about fostering values like transparency, collaboration, trust, and continuous improvement. Leaders and team members should promote these values and set an example for others to follow.

### 3.1.12. Change Management

Change management strategies should be employed to help individuals and teams adapt to Agile practices. Resistance to change should be addressed through clear communication, training, and support.

In conclusion, creating an Agile environment is a strategic step in preparing for a successful Scrum implementation. It requires leadership support, a shift in mindset, education, empowerment of teams, suitable tools and infrastructure, effective metrics, and the promotion of Agile values and culture. By investing in these foundational elements, organizations can set the stage for Agile methodologies like Scrum to flourish and drive improved project outcomes.

## 3.2. Introducing Scrum to Your Team

Introducing Scrum to your team is a significant step in adopting Agile practices. It involves educating your team about Scrum, aligning them with Agile principles, and transitioning to a new way of working. In this section, we will explore the key aspects of introducing Scrum to your team.

### 3.2.1. Scrum Basics

Start by introducing your team to the fundamental concepts of Scrum. This includes understanding the roles (Scrum Master, Product Owner, Development Team), Scrum events (Sprint, Sprint Planning, Daily Stand-up, Sprint Review, Sprint Retrospective), and artifacts (Product Backlog, Sprint Backlog, Increment).

### 3.2.2. Scrum Values

Emphasize the Scrum values of commitment, courage, focus, openness, and respect. These values form the foundation of the Scrum framework and guide team behavior and interactions.

### 3.2.3. Scrum Roles and Responsibilities

Explain the specific roles and responsibilities within a Scrum team:

- **Scrum Master:** Their role is to coach the team, remove impediments, and facilitate Scrum events.
- **Product Owner:** Responsible for defining and prioritizing the Product Backlog.
- **Development Team:** The cross-functional group responsible for delivering increments of potentially shippable product at the end of each Sprint.

### 3.2.4. Scrum Artifacts

Describe the Scrum artifacts:

- **Product Backlog:** A prioritized list of items that represent the work to be done.
- **Sprint Backlog:** A subset of the Product Backlog items selected for a Sprint.
- **Increment:** A potentially shippable product increment created during a Sprint.

### 3.2.5. Scrum Events

Detail the Scrum events:

- **Sprint:** A time-boxed period (usually 2-4 weeks) during which a potentially shippable product increment is created.
- **Sprint Planning:** A meeting at the beginning of the Sprint to plan the work to be done.
- **Daily Stand-up:** A brief daily meeting for the team to synchronize and plan the day's work.
- **Sprint Review:** A meeting at the end of the Sprint to inspect the increment and adapt the Product Backlog if needed.
- **Sprint Retrospective:** A meeting at the end of the Sprint for the team to reflect on their processes and identify improvements.

Introduce Scrum practices such as:

- **Prioritization:** How to prioritize items in the Product Backlog.
- **Estimation:** Techniques like Story Points or Ideal Days for estimating work.
- **Definition of Done (DoD):** Define the criteria that must be met for an item to be considered "done."



Highlight the flexibility of the Scrum framework. Scrum can be adapted to suit the team's needs and the specific project context. It is not a rigid set of rules but a framework that encourages inspection and adaptation.



Explain the Scrum Master's role in supporting the team, removing impediments, and fostering an environment of continuous improvement.



Develop a transition plan for moving from your current project management approach to Scrum. This plan should include timelines, training, and milestones for adopting Scrum.



Organize Scrum training and workshops for team members to gain hands-on experience and knowledge. This could include Scrum Master training, Product Owner training, and Developer training.



Consider starting with a pilot Scrum project to gain experience and build confidence in the Scrum framework. A pilot project allows the team to learn and adapt without the pressure of a full-scale transition.



Maintain open communication with team members throughout the transition. Keep them informed about changes, progress, and the reasons behind adopting Scrum. Encourage transparency in all aspects of work.



Provide ongoing coaching and support for the team as they implement Scrum. The Scrum Master plays a crucial role in guiding the team and addressing any challenges that arise.

### 3.2.14. Feedback and Adaptation

Collect feedback from team members and stakeholders regularly. Use this feedback to make adjustments to your Scrum implementation and improve the process continuously.

### 3.2.15. Celebrate Successes

Acknowledge and celebrate the achievements and successes that come from adopting Scrum. Recognize the team's efforts and the positive impact on project outcomes.

In summary, introducing Scrum to your team is a comprehensive process that involves education, training, cultural alignment, and a commitment to Agile principles. By taking a structured approach and providing the necessary support, organizations can successfully transition to Scrum and reap the benefits of improved project management and delivery.

---

## 3.3. Building a Collaborative Team Culture

Building a collaborative team culture is essential for the successful implementation of Scrum. Scrum relies on cross-functional teams working together to deliver value iteratively. In this section, we will explore the key elements of fostering a collaborative team culture within a Scrum environment.

### 3.3.1. Clear Goals and Objectives

Start by setting clear and well-defined goals and objectives for the team. Team members should have a shared understanding of what they are working towards. The Product Owner plays a crucial role in articulating the vision and goals through the Product Backlog.

### 3.3.2. Shared Responsibility

In a collaborative team culture, responsibility is shared among all team members. There is no "blame game" when things go wrong, and team members take ownership of both successes and failures. This creates a sense of accountability and mutual trust.

### 3.3.3. Open Communication

Open and transparent communication is the backbone of collaboration. Team members should feel comfortable expressing their thoughts, ideas, concerns, and feedback. Daily Stand-up meetings and Sprint Retrospectives provide opportunities for regular communication.

### 3.3.4. Active Listening

Active listening is a skill that team members should cultivate. It involves giving full attention to the speaker, asking clarifying questions, and seeking to understand before responding. Active listening fosters empathy and better comprehension within the team.

### 3.3.5. Cross-Functional Collaboration

Scrum teams are composed of cross-functional members with diverse skills. Encourage collaboration and knowledge sharing among team members. This diversity of skills and perspectives enriches problem-solving and decision-making.

### 3.3.6. Trust and Respect

Trust and respect are foundational to a collaborative culture. Team members should trust each other's capabilities and respect their opinions and contributions. Building trust takes time but is essential for a high-performing team.

### 3.3.7. Conflict Resolution

Conflicts are a natural part of team dynamics. The team should have established processes for resolving conflicts constructively. The Scrum Master can play a role in mediating conflicts and ensuring that they are addressed promptly.

### 3.3.8. Celebrating Success

Celebrate team successes, milestones, and achievements. Recognize individual contributions and team efforts. Celebrations foster a positive team spirit and motivation.

### 3.3.9. Embracing Diversity

Diverse teams bring different perspectives and approaches to problem-solving. Encourage inclusivity and embrace diversity within the team. It leads to innovative solutions and a richer team culture.

### 3.3.10. Empowering Team Members

Empower team members to make decisions and take ownership of their work. Give them the autonomy to self-organize and determine how best to achieve their Sprint goals.

### 3.3.11. Continuous Improvement

A culture of continuous improvement should be ingrained in the team's DNA. Regularly assess team processes, identify areas for improvement, and take action to implement changes. Sprint Retrospectives are an excellent forum for this.

### 3.3.12. Agile Principles

Reinforce Agile principles and values within the team. Encourage a focus on individuals and interactions, customer collaboration, responding to change, and delivering working solutions.

### 3.3.13. Mentorship and Learning

Promote mentorship and learning within the team. Experienced team members can mentor newcomers, helping them adapt to the team's culture and Agile practices.

Create an environment of psychological safety where team members feel safe to take risks, voice their opinions, and admit mistakes without fear of negative consequences. Psychological safety fosters innovation and open dialogue.



Leaders should support and model collaborative behaviors. Leaders can set an example by actively participating in Scrum events, listening to team members, and providing resources and support.

In conclusion, building a collaborative team culture is essential for the success of Scrum teams. It requires clear goals, shared responsibility, open communication, active listening, trust, and respect. By fostering a collaborative culture, organizations can maximize the effectiveness of their Scrum teams and deliver value more efficiently.

---

## 3.4. Essential Tools and Technologies for Scrum

In the world of Scrum, choosing the right tools and technologies can significantly impact the efficiency and effectiveness of your Agile teams. This section will explore the essential tools and technologies that support Scrum practices and help streamline project management and collaboration.

### 3.4.1. Scrum Software Tools

Scrum software tools are designed to facilitate Scrum ceremonies and processes. They often include features for managing the Product Backlog, Sprint planning, Daily Stand-ups, Sprint Reviews, and Sprint Retrospectives. Popular Scrum software tools include:

- **Jira:** Jira is a widely used Agile project management tool that supports Scrum. It allows you to create and manage user stories, plan Sprints, and track progress using customizable workflows.

- **Trello:** Trello provides a simple and visual way to manage tasks on boards. While it's versatile for various project management methods, it can be configured to support Scrum processes.

- **VersionOne:** VersionOne is a comprehensive Agile management platform that includes Scrum support. It offers features for backlog management, Sprint planning, and reporting.

- **Azure DevOps:** Azure DevOps, formerly known as Visual Studio Team Services (VSTS), provides tools for Agile project management and software development. It offers features for backlog management, release planning, and continuous integration.

- **Targetprocess:** Targetprocess is a visual project management tool that supports Scrum and other Agile frameworks. It provides customizable views and reporting for Scrum teams.

### 3.4.2. Collaboration and Communication Tools

Effective communication and collaboration are crucial for Scrum teams. Here are some tools that enhance team communication and collaboration:

- **Slack:** Slack is a popular team collaboration platform that offers real-time chat, file sharing, and integration with various other tools. It facilitates quick communication among team members.

- **Microsoft Teams:** Microsoft Teams is another collaboration platform that integrates with Microsoft Office 365. It provides chat, video conferencing, file sharing, and integration with other Microsoft tools.

- **Zoom:** Zoom is a widely used video conferencing tool that enables virtual meetings and collaboration, making it useful for distributed Scrum teams.

- **Confluence:** Confluence, developed by Atlassian, is a documentation and collaboration tool that allows teams to create, share, and collaborate on project documentation, meeting notes, and knowledge bases.

### 3.4.3. Version Control and Continuous Integration

Version control and continuous integration tools are essential for Scrum teams, especially in software development projects. These tools ensure code quality, version control, and automated testing:

- **Git:** Git is a distributed version control system widely used in software development. It allows teams to manage code, track changes, and collaborate on codebases.

- **GitHub:** GitHub is a web-based platform that hosts Git repositories and provides collaboration features like pull requests, code reviews, and issue tracking.

- **Bitbucket:** Bitbucket, also by Atlassian, offers Git and Mercurial repositories, along with features for code collaboration, continuous integration, and deployment.

- **Jenkins:** Jenkins is an open-source automation server that supports continuous integration and continuous delivery (CI/CD). It automates building, testing, and deploying applications.

### 3.4.4. Agile Metrics and Reporting Tools

To track progress and make data-driven decisions, Scrum teams need tools for agile metrics and reporting:

- **Tableau:** Tableau is a data visualization tool that helps teams create interactive and shareable dashboards and reports to monitor Agile project metrics.

- **Power BI:** Microsoft Power BI is a business analytics tool that allows teams to create visually compelling reports and dashboards from data sources.

- **Custom Reporting Tools:** Some organizations develop custom reporting tools or use built-in reporting features of their project management software to generate Agile metrics reports.

### 3.4.5. Task Management and Productivity Tools

Task management and productivity tools help Scrum teams stay organized and manage their work efficiently:

- **Asana:** Asana is a task and project management tool that helps teams plan, organize, and track work.

- **Monday.com:** Monday.com is a work operating system that enables teams to build custom workflows, track progress, and manage projects.

- **Toggl:** Toggl is a time tracking tool that helps teams analyze how they spend their time on different tasks and projects.

In conclusion, choosing the right tools and technologies is critical for the successful implementation of Scrum. These tools support various aspects of Scrum practices, from backlog management and Sprint planning to communication, collaboration, version control, and metrics tracking. The selection of tools should align with the specific needs and goals of your Scrum team and organization.

---

## 3.5. Overcoming Resistance to Scrum

Implementing Scrum often involves a significant change in how work is done, and change can be met with resistance. In this section, we will explore strategies for overcoming resistance to Scrum and ensuring a smoother transition.

### 3.5.1. Understand the Source of Resistance

To address resistance effectively, it's crucial to understand its source. Resistance can stem from various factors, such as fear of change, lack of understanding, concerns about job security, or previous negative experiences with Agile methodologies. Conduct interviews and surveys to identify the specific concerns within your organization.

### 3.5.2. Create a Clear Vision

Communicate a clear and compelling vision for why your organization is adopting Scrum. Highlight the benefits of Scrum, such as faster delivery of value, improved customer satisfaction, and enhanced team collaboration. Make sure everyone understands the "why" behind the change.

### 3.5.3. Leadership Alignment

Ensure that leadership is aligned with the Scrum adoption. Leaders should support and champion the change, setting an example for the rest of the organization. When leaders actively participate in Scrum events and demonstrate their commitment, it can reduce resistance.

### 3.5.4. Education and Training

Invest in education and training for all team members, including managers and stakeholders. Provide workshops and resources to help everyone understand Scrum principles and practices. Knowledge empowers individuals and reduces uncertainty.

### 3.5.5. Start Small

Consider starting with a small-scale Scrum implementation or pilot project. This allows teams to gain experience and confidence in Scrum without a massive disruption. Success in a pilot project can build momentum for broader adoption.

### 3.5.6. Address Misconceptions

Proactively address any misconceptions or myths about Scrum. Sometimes, resistance arises from misunderstandings or false information. Use clear communication and provide accurate information to dispel myths.

### 3.5.7. Involve Teams in the Change

Involve team members in the decision-making process and the design of Scrum processes. When individuals have a say in how Scrum is implemented, they are more likely to embrace the changes. Encourage teams to participate in process improvement and adapt Scrum to their needs.

### 3.5.8. Provide Support and Resources

Offer support and resources to teams as they transition to Scrum. This includes access to Scrum Masters, coaches, and mentors who can guide and support teams in their Agile journey. Ensure that teams have the necessary tools and infrastructure to work effectively.

### 3.5.9. Monitor Progress and Celebrate Wins

Regularly monitor the progress of Scrum adoption and celebrate small wins and achievements along the way. Recognize and reward teams for their efforts and improvements. Positive reinforcement can motivate teams to embrace Scrum fully.

Establish a continuous feedback loop for gathering input from team members and stakeholders. Create channels for individuals to express their concerns, provide feedback, and suggest improvements. Act on the feedback to make necessary adjustments.



Agile coaches and Scrum Masters play a vital role in addressing resistance. They can coach teams, facilitate discussions, and help individuals overcome challenges. Having experienced coaches can make a significant difference in the success of Scrum adoption.



Overcoming resistance to change takes time. Be patient and persistent in addressing concerns and challenges. Keep the lines of communication open and continue to reinforce the benefits of Scrum.



Regularly evaluate the effectiveness of your Scrum adoption strategy. If certain approaches are not working, be willing to adapt and try new strategies. Agile principles emphasize inspecting and adapting, and this applies to change management as well.

In conclusion, resistance to Scrum is a common challenge when implementing Agile practices. However, with the right strategies and a supportive organizational culture, it is possible to overcome resistance and successfully transition to Scrum. Understanding the source of resistance, providing education and training, involving teams in the change, and maintaining clear communication are key steps in addressing resistance effectively.

# Chapter 4: Sprint Planning and Execution

## 4.1. The Anatomy of a Sprint

Sprints are the heartbeat of Scrum, providing a time-boxed framework for teams to deliver value incrementally. In this section, we will dive into the essential elements that make up the anatomy of a Sprint.

### 4.1.1. Sprint Duration

A Sprint is a time-boxed period during which the Scrum team works to complete a set of product backlog items. Sprint durations typically range from 2 to 4 weeks, with the team selecting a duration that suits their work patterns and the nature of the project. Shorter Sprints provide more frequent opportunities for inspection and adaptation.

### 4.1.2. Sprint Goal

Each Sprint should have a clear and concise Sprint Goal. The Sprint Goal defines the purpose and expected outcome of the Sprint. It guides the team in making decisions about which product backlog items to work on and what to prioritize. The Sprint Goal serves as a unifying focus for the team throughout the Sprint.

### 4.1.3. Sprint Backlog

At the start of the Sprint, the team selects a set of product backlog items from the Product Backlog to work on. These selected items, along with any necessary tasks, make up the Sprint Backlog. The Sprint Backlog is a dynamic document that evolves as the team gains a better understanding of the work required.

### 4.1.4. Daily Stand-up

During the Sprint, the team holds a daily stand-up meeting, also known as the Daily Scrum. This short meeting is typically time-boxed to 15 minutes and provides an opportunity for team members to synchronize their work. Each team member answers three questions: What did I do yesterday? What will I do today? Are there any impediments blocking my progress?

### 4.1.5. Increment

The goal of each Sprint is to produce a potentially shippable Increment of the product. An Increment is a version of the product that is fully functional, meets the team's Definition of Done (DoD), and is potentially releasable. The Increment represents the value delivered at the end of the Sprint.

### 4.1.6. Scrum Events

Sprints are structured around key Scrum events, including Sprint Planning, Daily Stand-up, Sprint Review, and Sprint Retrospective. These events provide the framework for planning, inspecting progress, gathering feedback, and improving the team's processes.

### 4.1.7. Definition of Done (DoD)

The Definition of Done is a set of criteria that must be met for a product backlog item to be considered "done" and potentially releasable. It ensures that the Increment is of high quality and meets the team's standards. The DoD is a shared understanding within the team.

### 4.1.8. Sprint Burndown Chart

A Sprint Burndown Chart is a visual representation of the remaining work in the Sprint over time. It helps the team track their progress and assess whether they are on track to complete the Sprint Backlog within the Sprint duration. Burndown charts provide valuable insights into the team's velocity.

### 4.1.9. Inspect and Adapt

Throughout the Sprint, the Scrum team regularly inspects progress toward the Sprint Goal and adapts as necessary. They may discover changes in scope, encounter new information, or identify impediments. The ability to inspect and adapt is a fundamental aspect of Scrum.

### 4.1.10. Sprint Review

At the end of the Sprint, the team holds a Sprint Review meeting to demonstrate the Increment to stakeholders and gather feedback. The Sprint Review is an opportunity to assess whether the Increment meets the Sprint Goal and discuss any adjustments to the Product Backlog.

### 4.1.11. Sprint Retrospective

Following the Sprint Review, the team conducts a Sprint Retrospective to reflect on their processes and identify opportunities for improvement. The Retrospective is a time for the team to discuss what went well, what could be improved, and action items for the next Sprint.

### 4.1.12. Continuous Improvement

Sprints promote a culture of continuous improvement. Teams use the insights gained from Sprint Reviews and Retrospectives to make adjustments, enhance their processes, and increase their efficiency. The goal is to continuously deliver more value with each Sprint.

Once the Sprint Review and Sprint Retrospective are complete, the current Sprint is closed, and the team proceeds to plan the next Sprint. Any unresolved product backlog items are returned to the Product Backlog for prioritization in future Sprints.

In summary, the anatomy of a Sprint in Scrum involves a well-defined time-boxed period, a clear Sprint Goal, a dynamic Sprint Backlog, daily stand-up meetings, the production of a potentially shippable Increment, and a set of key Scrum events. It is within this structured framework that Scrum teams collaborate, deliver value, and continuously improve their work processes.

## 4.2. Effective Sprint Planning: Techniques and Best Practices

Sprint planning is a critical event in Scrum, as it sets the stage for the work to be accomplished during the upcoming Sprint. Effective sprint planning ensures that the Scrum team is aligned on the goals, scope, and tasks to be completed. In this section, we will explore techniques and best practices for conducting efficient and productive sprint planning meetings.

### 4.2.1. Preparing for Sprint Planning

Before the sprint planning meeting, there are several preparatory steps that the Scrum team should take:

- **Backlog Refinement:** The Product Owner should have prepared and refined the product backlog items that are candidates for the upcoming sprint. This includes breaking down user stories into smaller, manageable tasks, and ensuring that the items are well-defined and prioritized.

- **Definition of Done (DoD):** The team should have a clear and agreed-upon Definition of Done that outlines the criteria for a product backlog item to be considered complete. This ensures a shared understanding of what it means for work to be finished.

- **Capacity Planning:** The team should have a good understanding of their capacity for the upcoming sprint. This involves considering team velocity, holidays, and any other factors that might affect the team's availability during the sprint.

- **Sprint Goal:** The Product Owner and Scrum Master should work together to define a clear Sprint Goal. The Sprint Goal provides a unifying focus for the team and guides their work during the sprint.

The sprint planning meeting is a time-boxed event where the team collaboratively plans the work for the upcoming sprint. It typically consists of two parts:

*4.2.2.1. Part 1: What Can Be Done?*

In the first part of sprint planning, the team addresses the question, "What can be done in this sprint?" Here are some best practices for this phase:

- **Review the Sprint Goal:** Start by discussing the Sprint Goal, ensuring that everyone understands its significance and purpose.

- **Selecting Product Backlog Items:** The team collaboratively selects product backlog items from the top of the product backlog based on priority and the team's capacity. These selected items become the Sprint Backlog.

- **Breaking Down Tasks:** For each product backlog item selected, the team breaks down the work into smaller tasks or sub-tasks. This helps in creating a detailed plan for implementation.

- **Estimating Effort:** The team estimates the effort required for each task, typically using story points, hours, or other relevant units of measurement. This provides a basis for capacity planning.

- **Acceptance Criteria:** Ensure that each product backlog item has clear and well-defined acceptance criteria. These criteria define what it means for the work to be considered complete.

*4.2.2.2. Part 2: How Will It Be Done?*

In the second part of sprint planning, the team addresses the question, "How will the selected product backlog items be implemented?" Here are some best practices for this phase:

- **Task Assignment:** Assign tasks to individual team members based on their expertise and availability. Ensure that there is a shared understanding of who is responsible for each task.

- **Dependencies:** Discuss and identify any dependencies between tasks or product backlog items. Address how these dependencies will be managed during the sprint.

- **Capacity Planning:** Ensure that the team's capacity aligns with the selected work. If there is an imbalance between the team's capacity and the selected items, consider adjusting the scope or removing items from the sprint backlog.

- **Timeboxing:** Set time limits for discussions and decisions to keep the meeting on track and prevent over-analysis.

At the end of the sprint planning meeting, the team should have the following outcomes:

- A well-defined Sprint Backlog that includes selected product backlog items, tasks, and estimates.
- A shared understanding of the Sprint Goal and the work to be completed.
- Clarity on how the team plans to achieve the Sprint Goal.
- A commitment to the sprint backlog and a shared understanding of the scope.
- A plan for how the team will work together and collaborate during the sprint.

### 4.2.4. Continuous Improvement

Sprint planning is not a one-time event but an opportunity for continuous improvement. After each sprint, the team should reflect on the effectiveness of the planning process and look for ways to make it more efficient and collaborative.

In conclusion, effective sprint planning is essential for Scrum teams to deliver value efficiently and meet their Sprint Goals. It requires preparation, collaboration, and a shared commitment to the work ahead. By following best practices and continuously improving the sprint planning process, teams can enhance their productivity and alignment with Scrum principles.

---

## 4.3. Facilitating Daily Stand-ups

The Daily Stand-up, also known as the Daily Scrum, is a short and focused meeting that plays a vital role in Scrum by providing a regular opportunity for the team to synchronize and plan their work. In this section, we will delve into the details of facilitating effective Daily Stand-up meetings.

### 4.3.1. The Purpose of the Daily Stand-up

The Daily Stand-up serves several essential purposes within Scrum:

1. **Synchronization:** It helps team members synchronize their activities by sharing updates on what they worked on, what they plan to work on, and any obstacles they are facing.

2. **Daily Planning:** It supports daily planning by allowing team members to collaboratively decide on the tasks they will focus on during the day, ensuring alignment with the Sprint Goal.

3. **Transparency:** It promotes transparency within the team by providing visibility into individual and collective progress, facilitating open communication.

4. **Identifying Impediments:** It allows team members to identify and discuss any impediments or obstacles that are hindering their progress, enabling timely problem-solving.



The Daily Stand-up primarily involves three roles:

- **Development Team:** Team members report on their progress and plans during the Sprint. They share what they accomplished since the last Daily Stand-up, what they plan to do next, and any impediments they are facing.

- **Scrum Master:** The Scrum Master facilitates the Daily Stand-up but does not own it. They ensure that the meeting stays focused, time-boxed, and follows the agenda. The Scrum Master may help remove impediments or facilitate discussions if needed.

- **Product Owner:** The Product Owner may attend the Daily Stand-up as an observer but does not typically participate directly. Their presence allows them to understand the team's progress and priorities.



To facilitate an effective Daily Stand-up, consider the following guidelines:

- **Time-Boxing:** Keep the meeting time-boxed to 15 minutes or less to ensure it remains concise and focused.

- **Physical Presence:** Encourage team members to be physically present in the same location whenever possible. However, for distributed teams, virtual stand-ups are acceptable.

- **Standing:** Encourage team members to stand during the meeting to promote brevity and discourage excessive discussion.

- **Three Questions:** Each team member should answer three standard questions:

    1. What did I do yesterday?
    2. What will I do today?
    3. Are there any impediments or blockers?

- **Focus on Commitment:** Emphasize commitment rather than status reporting. Team members should commit to specific tasks for the day.

- **Impediment Resolution:** If someone raises an impediment, it is the Scrum Master's responsibility to ensure that it is addressed promptly, even if it means scheduling a separate discussion.

- **No Problem Solving:** While the Daily Stand-up is a place to identify impediments, it is not the forum for problem-solving discussions. Those should be handled outside the meeting.

- **Participation:** Ensure that all team members actively participate and that no one dominates the conversation. The Scrum Master may intervene if necessary to maintain balance.

- **Non-Blocking:** Focus on blockers or impediments that are preventing progress. Avoid discussing routine updates or status reports.

- **Visual Aids:** Some teams find it helpful to use visual aids such as a task board or digital tools to track progress and make the meeting more interactive.

- **Continuous Improvement:** Periodically review and reflect on the effectiveness of the Daily Stand-up and make adjustments as needed. Continuous improvement is a core principle of Scrum.

### 4.3.4. Pitfalls to Avoid

Facilitating Daily Stand-ups effectively also involves avoiding common pitfalls:

- **Becoming a Status Meeting:** Avoid allowing the Daily Stand-up to devolve into a status meeting where team members provide lengthy updates. It should focus on planning and impediment removal.

- **Late Start:** Ensure that the meeting starts promptly at the agreed-upon time, even if some team members are running late. Punctuality helps maintain discipline.

- **Lack of Engagement:** Encourage active participation from all team members. If some members are disengaged or not contributing, address this issue outside the meeting.

- **Discussion of Technical Details:** Avoid getting into deep technical discussions during the Daily Stand-up. Save those discussions for separate meetings if necessary.

- **Blame or Finger-Pointing:** Foster a blame-free environment. If problems are identified, focus on solutions and collaboration rather than assigning blame.

In conclusion, the Daily Stand-up is a core Scrum practice that promotes synchronization, planning, transparency, and problem-solving within the team. Effective facilitation of this daily meeting requires adherence to time-boxing, adherence to the three standard questions, a focus on commitment, and the avoidance of common pitfalls. By following these guidelines, teams can ensure that their Daily Stand-ups remain valuable and efficient.

## 4.4. Maintaining Momentum During Sprints

Maintaining momentum throughout a Sprint is crucial for a Scrum team to achieve its Sprint Goal and deliver a valuable Increment. In this section, we will explore strategies and best practices for keeping the team energized and focused during the course of a Sprint.

### 4.4.1. The Importance of Momentum

Momentum in a Sprint refers to the team's ability to sustain a consistent pace of work and progress toward completing the Sprint Goal. When momentum is maintained, the team is more likely to deliver a potentially shippable product Increment by the end of the Sprint. Here are some key reasons why momentum is vital:

- **Predictable Delivery:** Maintaining momentum helps the team deliver a predictable amount of work by the end of each Sprint, allowing stakeholders to plan accordingly.

- **Quality and Collaboration:** Consistent progress fosters a culture of quality and collaboration within the team. Team members remain engaged and focused on delivering value.

- **Motivation:** Achieving small victories throughout the Sprint keeps team members motivated and engaged. It provides a sense of accomplishment and satisfaction.

- **Risk Reduction:** Momentum reduces the risk of work being left incomplete at the end of the Sprint, which could lead to a failed Sprint or compromised Increment.

### 4.4.2. Strategies for Maintaining Momentum

To maintain momentum during a Sprint, Scrum teams can implement the following strategies and best practices:

#### 4.4.2.1. Sprint Planning Clarity

At the beginning of the Sprint, ensure that the Sprint Goal and the selected product backlog items are well-defined and understood by the entire team. Clear objectives help the team stay focused and motivated throughout the Sprint.

#### 4.4.2.2. Daily Stand-ups

Effective Daily Stand-up meetings are crucial for maintaining momentum. Encourage team members to share their progress, plans, and impediments daily. Identify and address any roadblocks promptly to prevent them from derailing the team's progress.

#### 4.4.2.3. Task Breakdown

Break down product backlog items into smaller, manageable tasks with clear acceptance criteria. This allows team members to work on specific tasks and make incremental progress, contributing to overall momentum.

Assign ownership of tasks to individual team members. When individuals take ownership of their tasks, they are more likely to maintain focus and accountability.



Encourage time management techniques such as timeboxing and Pomodoro sessions to help team members stay on track and make the most of their work time.



Foster a collaborative work environment where team members actively communicate, share knowledge, and support each other. Collaboration helps resolve issues quickly and keeps work moving forward.



Ensure that the team does not overcommit to work in the Sprint. Overcommitment can lead to stress and a loss of momentum. The team should have a realistic understanding of its capacity.



Continuously inspect progress against the Sprint Goal and the Sprint Backlog. If the team is falling behind or facing unexpected challenges, adapt the plan and seek solutions proactively.



Recognize and celebrate small achievements and milestones reached during the Sprint. Acknowledging progress boosts team morale and reinforces the importance of maintaining momentum.



During the Sprint Review, focus on the Increment's value and how it aligns with the Sprint Goal. This reinforces the importance of the Sprint Goal and the need to maintain momentum.



Gather insights and feedback during the Sprint Retrospective. Use this information to make improvements that can enhance the team's ability to maintain momentum in future Sprints.

### 4.4.3. Common Challenges and Solutions

Maintaining momentum can be challenging due to various factors such as unforeseen impediments, changing priorities, or team dynamics. Here are some common challenges and potential solutions:

- **Impediments:** Address impediments promptly, involve the Scrum Master and the team, and seek solutions collaboratively.

- **Changing Priorities:** Ensure that changes in priorities are communicated clearly and that the team has a process for handling them without losing momentum.

- **Burnout:** Watch for signs of burnout among team members and encourage a healthy work-life balance.

- **Scope Creep:** Prevent scope creep by adhering to the Definition of Done and regularly inspecting the Sprint Backlog.

- **Lack of Motivation:** Foster a motivating work environment, and recognize and reward achievements to boost motivation.

### 4.4.4. Continuous Improvement

As with all Scrum practices, maintaining momentum is subject to continuous improvement. After each Sprint, the team should reflect on what went well and what can be improved regarding momentum. This reflection and adaptation are essential for achieving higher levels of performance and predictability in future Sprints.

In conclusion, maintaining momentum during Sprints is crucial for Scrum teams to consistently deliver value and achieve their Sprint Goals. It involves a combination of clear planning, effective communication, collaboration, time management, and a focus on problem-solving. By implementing these strategies and continuously improving

---

## 4.5. Handling Impediments and Blocks

In the world of Scrum, impediments and blocks are hurdles that can slow down or even halt a team's progress. Handling these impediments effectively is crucial to ensure that the team can continue to work efficiently and meet their Sprint Goal. In this section, we'll explore the significance of identifying, addressing, and preventing impediments in Scrum.

### 4.5.1. Understanding Impediments and Blocks

Impediments and blocks are obstacles that hinder a team's progress or prevent them from completing their work. These obstacles can take various forms, including:

- **Technical Challenges:** Issues related to software, hardware, or infrastructure that impede development work.

- **Dependency Delays:** When a team is waiting for external dependencies, such as APIs or third-party components, to be completed.

- **Lack of Information:** Teams may lack essential information, requirements, or clarifications needed to proceed with their tasks.

- **Resource Constraints:** Insufficient resources, including team members or equipment, can slow down work.

- **Organizational Issues:** Problems related to the organization's structure, policies, or culture that impact the team's ability to work effectively.

### 4.5.2. Identifying Impediments

Identifying impediments is the first step in addressing them. Teams can use several methods to identify impediments:

- **Daily Stand-up:** The Daily Stand-up is an excellent opportunity for team members to raise any impediments they encounter.

- **Impediment Backlog:** Some teams maintain an "Impediment Backlog" or a list of obstacles that need to be addressed. This provides visibility into ongoing impediments.

- **Feedback Loops:** Encourage team members to provide feedback and share any challenges they face during their work.

- **Scrum Master's Role:** The Scrum Master plays a crucial role in identifying and addressing impediments. They should actively listen to the team and be aware of potential roadblocks.

- **Regular Inspections:** Regularly inspecting the team's progress and their Sprint Backlog can reveal impediments that need attention.

### 4.5.3. Addressing Impediments

Once identified, impediments should be addressed promptly to prevent them from affecting the team's progress. Here's a structured approach to addressing impediments:

1. **Capture:** Document the impediment in a clear and concise manner. Include details such as its nature, impact, and any relevant context.

2. **Prioritize:** Assess the urgency and impact of the impediment and prioritize it accordingly. High-impact and urgent impediments should be addressed first.

3. **Ownership:** Assign ownership of the impediment to a responsible individual or team member. This person will be accountable for finding a solution or escalating the issue.

4. **Resolution:** Work collaboratively to find a solution to the impediment. This may involve brainstorming, troubleshooting, or seeking help from others.

5.  **Escalation:** If the impediment cannot be resolved within the team's capacity or expertise, escalate it to the relevant stakeholders or higher authorities.

6.  **Follow-Up:** Regularly follow up on the status of the impediment to ensure that progress is being made toward its resolution.



While addressing impediments is essential, preventing them is equally valuable. Here are some strategies for preventing impediments:

- **Proactive Communication:** Foster a culture of proactive communication within the team. Encourage team members to raise potential issues early, even before they become full-blown impediments.

- **Cross-Functional Teams:** Ensure that the team is cross-functional, with a diverse set of skills. This can help mitigate potential resource constraints.

- **Clear Requirements:** Invest time in clarifying requirements and user stories before they are added to the Sprint Backlog. This reduces the likelihood of missing information becoming an impediment.

- **Dependency Management:** Manage dependencies effectively by identifying them early and collaborating with external teams or stakeholders to minimize delays.

- **Regular Retrospectives:** Use Sprint Retrospectives to discuss and address recurring impediments. Teams can brainstorm solutions and make process improvements to prevent similar issues in the future.

- **Scrum Master's Role:** Empower the Scrum Master to actively monitor and address impediments. They can act as a facilitator, coach, and advocate for the team's needs.



When addressing impediments, teams should be cautious of common pitfalls, such as:

- **Ignoring Impediments:** Ignoring or downplaying impediments can lead to project delays and dissatisfaction among team members.

- **Overreacting:** On the other hand, overreacting to every minor issue can lead to unnecessary disruptions. Teams should strike a balance.

- **Lack of Follow-Up:** Failing to follow up on the status of impediments can result in unresolved issues lingering.

- **Blame Game:** Teams should avoid assigning blame when addressing impediments. Instead, focus on finding solutions and preventing future occurrences.

- **Incomplete Documentation:** Inadequate documentation of impediments can lead to misunderstandings and hinder their resolution.

Handling impediments and blocks is a continuous improvement process. Teams should regularly review their impediment-handling practices and look for ways to become more effective. This might include refining their documentation, improving communication, or streamlining their escalation procedures.

In conclusion, effectively handling impediments and blocks is vital for Scrum teams to maintain their productivity and progress toward their Sprint Goal. By identifying, addressing, and preventing impediments systematically, teams can work more efficiently and deliver value consistently. Additionally, embracing a culture of continuous improvement ensures that impediment-handling practices evolve over time for the betterment of the team.

# Chapter 5: The Art of Backlog Management

## 5.1. Understanding the Product Backlog

The Product Backlog is a foundational element of Scrum, serving as the single source of truth for a product's requirements, features, enhancements, and fixes. In this section, we will delve into the significance of the Product Backlog, its characteristics, and how it drives the work of a Scrum team.

### 5.1.1. What Is the Product Backlog?

The Product Backlog is a prioritized list of all the work that needs to be done for a product. It encompasses all potential features, user stories, bug fixes, technical tasks, and improvements that could be part of the product's future iterations.

### 5.1.2. Characteristics of the Product Backlog

1. *Dynamic: The Product Backlog is dynamic and evolves over time. It is not a fixed or static document. New items can be added, and existing items can be reprioritized or removed as the product evolves and stakeholders' needs change.*

2. *Prioritized: The items in the Product Backlog are prioritized based on their value to the product and its stakeholders. Higher-priority items are at the top, and lower-priority items are further down the list.*

3. *Detailed: Each item in the Product Backlog should contain sufficient detail for the development team to understand it. This typically includes a description, acceptance criteria, and any relevant attachments or mockups.*

4. *Estimable: Items in the Product Backlog should be estimable, meaning the team can provide a reasonable estimate of the effort required to complete them. This helps with Sprint planning.*

5. *Negotiable: The details of items in the Product Backlog are negotiable. This means that as the team learns more or as priorities change, the details can be adjusted through collaboration with stakeholders.*

6. *Value-Driven: The Product Backlog is driven by value. Items at the top of the backlog should deliver the most value to the product and its users.*

### 5.1.3. Ownership of the Product Backlog

The Product Backlog is owned by the Product Owner, who is responsible for its creation, maintenance, and prioritization. The Product Owner collaborates with stakeholders to gather input and insights, ensuring that the backlog reflects the needs of the product's users and the organization.

### 5.1.4. Grooming the Product Backlog

Product Backlog grooming, also known as backlog refinement, is an ongoing activity in Scrum. It involves reviewing and refining the items in the backlog to ensure that they are well-defined, properly prioritized, and ready for the development team to work on in upcoming Sprints.

During backlog grooming sessions, the team and the Product Owner collaborate to:

- **Add Detail:** Add more detail to backlog items as needed, including clear acceptance criteria and any necessary attachments.

- **Estimate:** Estimate the effort required to complete each backlog item. This helps with Sprint planning and ensures that items are appropriately sized.

- **Re-Prioritize:** Adjust the order of backlog items based on changes in business priorities, user feedback, or new insights.

- **Remove Obsolete Items:** Remove items that are no longer relevant or necessary for the product's development.

### 5.1.5. Role of the Development Team

While the Product Owner is responsible for the Product Backlog, the development team also plays a role in its management. They provide input during grooming sessions, seek clarification on backlog items, and help ensure that items are well-defined and feasible.

### 5.1.6. Using User Stories in the Product Backlog

User stories are a common format for expressing items in the Product Backlog. A user story typically follows the "As a [user], I want [feature/ability] so that [benefit/value]" format. User stories focus on the user's perspective and the value delivered.

Here's an example of a user story:

- As a website visitor,
- I want to easily reset my password
- So that I can regain access to my account if I forget my password.

User stories help maintain a user-centric view of the product's functionality and allow the team to prioritize work based on user needs.

### 5.1.7. Summary

The Product Backlog is a dynamic, prioritized, and detailed list of all work that needs to be done for a product. It plays a central role in Scrum, serving as the primary source of requirements and guiding the team's work during Sprint planning. The Product Owner is responsible for its management, including grooming and prioritization, with input from the development team and stakeholders. By maintaining a well-groomed and value-driven

Product Backlog, a Scrum team can ensure that they are consistently delivering value to their users and stakeholders.

---

## 5.2. Prioritization Techniques for the Backlog

Prioritizing items in the Product Backlog is a critical aspect of successful Scrum implementation. It ensures that the team works on the most valuable and important features first, delivering maximum benefit to the product and its stakeholders. In this section, we will explore various prioritization techniques commonly used in Scrum.

### 5.2.1. Why Prioritization Matters

Prioritization is essential for several reasons:

1. **Maximizing Value:** It helps the team focus on delivering high-value features and improvements early in the product's development, ensuring that the most critical needs are addressed first.

2. **Alignment with Goals:** Prioritization ensures that the team's work aligns with the overall goals and objectives of the product and the organization.

3. **Risk Reduction:** Addressing critical items early can reduce project risks, uncover potential issues sooner, and provide opportunities for course correction.

4. **Stakeholder Satisfaction:** Prioritizing based on stakeholder feedback helps ensure that their needs and expectations are met, leading to higher satisfaction.

5. **Efficient Resource Allocation:** It optimizes the allocation of the team's resources, ensuring that they are working on the most valuable tasks.

### 5.2.2. Common Prioritization Techniques

#### 1. MoSCoW Method

The MoSCoW method categorizes backlog items into four priority levels:

- **Must-Have:** Items that are critical and must be included in the next release or Sprint.

- **Should-Have:** Important items that should be included but can be deferred if necessary.

- **Could-Have:** Desirable items that could be included if time and resources permit.

- **Won't-Have:** Items that are not included in the current scope but may be considered for future releases.

## 2. Value vs. Effort (ICE)

The ICE prioritization technique involves assigning scores to backlog items based on their perceived value, effort, and confidence. Each item is given a score, and items with higher scores are prioritized.

- **Impact:** How much value will this item deliver?

- **Confidence:** How certain are we about the estimates for this item?

- **Effort:** How much effort will it take to complete this item?

The formula for calculating ICE score is Impact × Confidence ÷ Effort.

## 3. Relative Weighting

Relative weighting involves comparing items in pairs and determining which one is more important. This technique is often used in combination with other methods.

## 4. Kano Model

The Kano model categorizes features into three categories:

- **Basic Needs:** Features that are expected by users and don't necessarily provide a competitive advantage when implemented. They are prerequisites for user satisfaction.

- **Performance Needs:** Features that can enhance user satisfaction linearly with their implementation.

- **Excitement Needs:** Features that delight users when implemented but don't necessarily lead to dissatisfaction if missing.

This model helps prioritize features based on their impact on user satisfaction.

## 5. Business Value Poker

In this technique, stakeholders or team members assign a value (e.g., monetary value) to each backlog item independently and anonymously. They discuss any significant discrepancies in values and reach a consensus on prioritization.

## 6. Buy a Feature

Stakeholders are given a budget, and they "buy" the features they want to see in the next release. This technique encourages stakeholders to make trade-offs and prioritize based on their budget constraints.

RICE (Reach, Impact, Confidence, and Effort) is another scoring method for prioritization. It considers how many users will be reached, the impact on each user, the confidence in the estimates, and the effort required.

## 5.2.3. Choosing the Right Technique

The choice of prioritization technique depends on the specific needs of the project, the nature of the backlog items, and the preferences of the Scrum team and stakeholders. In some cases, a combination of techniques may be used to ensure a well-rounded prioritization process.

## 5.2.4. Ongoing Prioritization

Prioritization is not a one-time activity. It is an ongoing process, and the backlog should be reviewed and reprioritized regularly. Changes in market conditions, stakeholder feedback, and emerging insights may necessitate adjustments to the backlog priorities.

In conclusion, effective backlog prioritization is crucial for Scrum teams to deliver the most valuable work first. The choice of prioritization technique depends on the project's context and goals. Regularly revisiting and adjusting backlog priorities ensures that the team remains aligned with stakeholder needs and focused on delivering maximum value.

---

## 5.3. Backlog Grooming Sessions

Backlog grooming, also known as backlog refinement, is a vital and recurring activity in Scrum that ensures the Product Backlog is well-prepared and ready for Sprint planning. In this section, we will delve into the purpose, benefits, and best practices of backlog grooming sessions.

### 5.3.1. Purpose of Backlog Grooming

The primary purpose of backlog grooming is to maintain a Product Backlog that is clear, detailed, and prioritized so that the Scrum team can effectively plan and execute their Sprints. Here are the key objectives:

1. **Clarity:** Grooming sessions aim to clarify backlog items, ensuring that they are well-defined, have clear acceptance criteria, and are understood by the team.

2. **Prioritization:** The team reviews and adjusts the priorities of backlog items based on changes in business needs, feedback, and new insights.

3. **Estimation:** During grooming, the team estimates the effort required to complete backlog items, helping with Sprint planning and capacity management.

4. **Remove Ambiguities:** Any ambiguity or uncertainty around backlog items is addressed, reducing the risk of misunderstandings during development.

5. **Refinement:** Grooming provides an opportunity to refine user stories, tasks, and acceptance criteria to ensure they are actionable for the team.

### 5.3.2. Benefits of Backlog Grooming

Effective backlog grooming offers several benefits:

- **Improved Sprint Planning:** A well-groomed backlog makes Sprint planning more efficient and accurate, as the team can confidently select and commit to a set of backlog items.

- **Reduced Waste:** Grooming helps prevent the team from working on items that are not well-defined or lack clarity, reducing rework and waste.

- **Increased Productivity:** By addressing uncertainties and dependencies early, grooming reduces interruptions and roadblocks during Sprints, leading to increased productivity.

- **Better Collaboration:** Grooming sessions encourage collaboration between the Product Owner and the development team, fostering a shared understanding of the product's goals and requirements.

- **Higher Quality Deliverables:** Clear, well-defined backlog items result in higher-quality deliverables, as the team knows what is expected.

### 5.3.3. Who Should Attend Grooming Sessions?

Backlog grooming is a collaborative activity that involves key Scrum roles:

1. **Product Owner:** The Product Owner is responsible for leading grooming sessions, providing context, and answering questions about backlog items.

2. **Development Team:** Team members actively participate in grooming sessions, seeking clarification, estimating effort, and providing input on technical feasibility.

3. **Scrum Master:** The Scrum Master facilitates the grooming process, ensuring that it is effective and that Scrum practices are followed.

4. **Stakeholders:** Depending on the organization, stakeholders may be invited to grooming sessions to provide input and clarify requirements.

### 5.3.4. How Often Should Grooming Sessions Occur?

The frequency of backlog grooming sessions can vary depending on the project's needs but typically occurs on a regular basis, often once a Sprint. These sessions may be shorter and less formal than Sprint planning meetings but are essential to maintaining a healthy backlog.

To make backlog grooming sessions productive, consider the following best practices:

1. **Preparation:** The Product Owner should come prepared with backlog items that need attention, including new items and those that require refinement or re-prioritization.

2. **Time-Boxing:** Set a time limit for grooming sessions to keep them focused and prevent them from becoming overly lengthy.

3. **Collaboration:** Encourage open communication and collaboration among team members and stakeholders to ensure a shared understanding of backlog items.

4. **Priority Review:** Regularly review and adjust backlog item priorities based on changing circumstances and stakeholder feedback.

5. **Estimation:** Use estimation techniques like Planning Poker to estimate the effort required for backlog items.

6. **Documentation:** Keep records of discussions and decisions made during grooming sessions for future reference.

### 5.3.6. Summary

Backlog grooming is a vital Scrum practice that ensures the Product Backlog is well-prepared and ready for Sprint planning. By maintaining a clear, prioritized, and detailed backlog, teams can work more efficiently, reduce waste, and deliver higher-quality products. Collaboration among the Product Owner, development team, Scrum Master, and stakeholders is key to successful backlog grooming, and it should occur regularly to keep the backlog in optimal condition.

---

## 5.4. User Stories and Estimation

User stories are a fundamental concept in Scrum and agile development. They serve as a way to express the requirements and expectations of the users in a simple and understandable manner. In this section, we will explore what user stories are, how to write them effectively, and the estimation of user story points.

### 5.4.1. What Are User Stories?

A user story is a concise, informal description of a feature, requirement, or piece of functionality from the perspective of an end-user or customer. It is typically written in a user-centric format, following the structure: "As a [user], I want [feature] so that [benefit/value]."

For example, a user story for an e-commerce website might be:

- As a registered customer,
- I want to be able to save items in my shopping cart
- So that I can complete my purchase at a later time without losing my selections.

User stories are often written on index cards or in digital tools and serve as a lightweight way to capture and communicate requirements.

## 5.4.2. Characteristics of User Stories

Effective user stories exhibit the following characteristics:

- **Independent:** User stories should be self-contained and not dependent on other stories. This allows for flexibility in prioritization and development.

- **Negotiable:** Details of a user story are negotiable and can be discussed and refined during grooming and Sprint planning.

- **Valuable:** Each user story should deliver value to the end-user or customer. It should solve a real problem or provide a benefit.

- **Estimable:** Team members should be able to estimate the effort required to complete a user story. This aids in Sprint planning.

- **Small:** User stories should be small enough to be completed within a single Sprint, typically ranging from a few hours to a few days of work.

- **Testable:** There should be clear acceptance criteria that define when a user story is considered done and meets the user's expectations.

## 5.4.3. Writing Effective User Stories

To write effective user stories, consider the following tips:

- **User-Centric:** Always focus on the user and their needs. Use the "As a [user]…" format to keep the user at the center of the story.

- **Benefit-Oriented:** Describe the benefit or value that the user will gain from the feature. This helps prioritize stories based on their impact.

- **Clear and Concise:** Keep user stories simple and easy to understand. Avoid unnecessary technical details or jargon.

- **Independent:** Ensure that each user story is independent and can be implemented without relying on other stories.

- **Testable Acceptance Criteria:** Include clear and testable acceptance criteria that define what it means for the story to be complete and meet the user's expectations.

Estimation is an important part of Scrum, helping teams plan their work and allocate resources effectively. User story points are a common way to estimate the effort required to complete user stories. Here's how it works:

- Teams assign points to user stories based on their perceived complexity, effort, and risk. The Fibonacci sequence (1, 2, 3, 5, 8, 13, etc.) or other point scales are often used.

- Teams use historical data and their collective judgment to assign points. They may also consider factors like technical challenges, dependencies, and unknowns.

- Estimation is a collaborative effort, involving team members and often using techniques like Planning Poker to reach a consensus.

- User story points are a relative measure, helping teams understand the relative size of stories. They are not a measure of time but rather complexity.

- During Sprint planning, teams select a certain number of user story points to work on based on their capacity.



Velocity is a metric used in Scrum to measure a team's capacity and productivity. It represents the number of story points a team can complete in a Sprint. Over time, teams can use their velocity to plan future Sprints more accurately.

During the first few Sprints, teams may struggle to estimate accurately, but as they gain experience, their velocity becomes more predictable.



User stories are not static; they may need refinement and re-estimation as more details become available or the team's understanding evolves. This happens during backlog grooming sessions when the team and Product Owner collaboratively update and clarify stories.

In conclusion, user stories are a vital tool for expressing requirements in a user-centric and understandable manner. They are characterized by their independence, negotiability, value, estimability, small size, and testability. Estimating user story points helps teams plan their work, and velocity is used to measure productivity and guide Sprint planning. Regular refinement and re-estimation ensure that user stories remain effective throughout the development process.

## 5.5. Collaborating with the Product Owner

Collaboration between the Scrum team and the Product Owner is a cornerstone of successful Scrum projects. In this section, we will delve into the importance of collaboration with the Product Owner, the role of the Product Owner, and best practices for effective collaboration.

### 5.5.1. The Role of the Product Owner

The Product Owner (PO) is a crucial member of the Scrum team responsible for defining and prioritizing the Product Backlog. Their primary role is to represent the voice of the customer or end-users and make decisions that maximize the value of the product.

Key responsibilities of the Product Owner include:

- **Defining User Stories:** The PO works with stakeholders to gather and document requirements in the form of user stories. They ensure that user stories are clear, concise, and prioritize them based on business value.

- **Prioritizing the Backlog:** The PO decides the order in which user stories are tackled, taking into account business goals, user needs, and market conditions.

- **Acceptance Criteria:** They define the acceptance criteria for user stories, which specify when a user story is considered complete and meets the user's expectations.

- **Answering Questions:** The PO is available to the development team during Sprint execution to answer questions, provide clarifications, and make decisions.

- **Accepting or Rejecting Work:** At the end of each Sprint, the PO reviews the completed work and accepts or rejects it based on whether it meets the acceptance criteria.

### 5.5.2. Importance of Collaboration

Effective collaboration with the Product Owner is critical for several reasons:

- **Shared Vision:** Collaborating with the PO ensures that the development team shares a common understanding of the product's vision and goals.

- **Alignment:** Regular communication with the PO helps the team stay aligned with business priorities and user needs, making it more likely to deliver value.

- **Clarification:** The PO can provide clarification and guidance to the team during development, reducing misunderstandings and rework.

- **Feedback Loop:** Collaboration allows for a continuous feedback loop, enabling the team to adapt to changing requirements and priorities.

- **Empowerment:** Collaborating with the PO empowers the team to make informed decisions and prioritize work effectively.

To foster effective collaboration with the Product Owner, consider the following best practices:

1. **Regular Communication:** Maintain open and frequent communication with the PO, including daily stand-up meetings and backlog grooming sessions.

2. **User Story Workshops:** Conduct user story workshops or refinement sessions where the team and PO collectively define and clarify user stories.

3. **Acceptance Criteria Review:** Review and confirm acceptance criteria with the PO before starting work on a user story to ensure a shared understanding of expectations.

4. **Collaborative Tools:** Use collaborative tools for backlog management, such as digital boards or project management software, to facilitate communication and transparency.

5. **Feedback Loops:** Encourage the PO to provide feedback on completed work during Sprint reviews and retrospectives to identify areas for improvement.

6. **Empower the Team:** Empower the development team to ask questions, seek clarifications, and make decisions when the PO is unavailable.

7. **Respect Roles:** Respect the roles and responsibilities of both the development team and the PO, understanding that the PO provides direction and the team implements the work.



Collaboration with the Product Owner may face challenges such as conflicting priorities, unclear requirements, or communication barriers. It is essential to address these challenges proactively through open and honest communication and by using agile practices like backlog grooming and Sprint reviews to refine and clarify requirements.

In conclusion, collaborating effectively with the Product Owner is essential for successful Scrum projects. The Product Owner plays a pivotal role in defining, prioritizing, and clarifying requirements, while the development team implements the work. Regular communication, shared understanding, and a collaborative mindset are key to achieving the goals of Scrum and delivering value to the customer.

## Section 6.1: Preparing for the Sprint Review

Sprint reviews are essential ceremonies in the Scrum framework, providing an opportunity for the Scrum team to showcase the work completed during the sprint. This section focuses on the preparations needed for a successful sprint review.

*The Importance of Sprint Reviews*

Before delving into the preparations, it's crucial to understand why sprint reviews are significant. Sprint reviews serve several purposes:

1. **Transparency**: Sprint reviews provide transparency to stakeholders, allowing them to see the progress made by the Scrum team.

2. **Feedback Gathering**: They offer a platform for stakeholders to provide feedback on the increment developed during the sprint.

3. **Learning**: Sprint reviews encourage continuous learning by evaluating what went well and what could be improved.

4. **Product Demonstration**: They include a product demonstration, showcasing the potentially shippable product increment.

*Preparing the Product Increment*

To ensure a successful sprint review, the Scrum team should focus on preparing the product increment. This involves:

- **Functional Product**: The product increment should be functional, meeting the Definition of Done (DoD) criteria.

- **User Stories**: Ensure that user stories and product backlog items selected for the sprint are completed.

- **Testing**: Thoroughly test the increment to identify and address any defects or issues.

- **Documentation**: Prepare necessary documentation such as user manuals or release notes.

*Inviting Stakeholders*

Another critical aspect of sprint review preparation is inviting the right stakeholders. This includes:

- **Product Owner**: The Product Owner is a key participant who ensures that the increment aligns with the product vision and objectives.

- **Development Team**: All members of the development team should be present to explain their contributions.

- **Scrum Master**: The Scrum Master facilitates the review but also participates as a member of the team.

- **Stakeholders**: Invite relevant stakeholders such as customers, end-users, and managers who can provide valuable input.



A well-structured agenda ensures that the sprint review stays on track. Consider the following components:

- **Introduction**: Start with a brief introduction, welcoming attendees and explaining the purpose of the review.

- **Product Demonstration**: Showcase the product increment, highlighting its features and functionalities.

- **Feedback and Questions**: Open the floor for feedback and questions from stakeholders.

- **Review of Sprint Goals**: Discuss whether the sprint goals were met and any changes to the product backlog.

- **Action Items**: Identify action items and improvements for the next sprint.



In some cases, visual aids or presentation materials can enhance the understanding of the product. These materials might include:

- **Charts and Graphs**: Use charts or graphs to illustrate progress, velocity, or other relevant metrics.

- **Screenshots**: Include screenshots or visuals to showcase specific features or changes.

- **User Stories**: Share user stories or personas to provide context for the work completed.



The Scrum Master plays a crucial role in facilitating the sprint review. They should:

- **Ensure Inclusivity**: Encourage active participation from all attendees, giving everyone a chance to speak.

- **Time Management**: Keep the review within the timebox to respect participants' schedules.

- **Focus on Objectives**: Ensure the discussion remains focused on the sprint review objectives.



Effective sprint review preparation is vital for a successful and productive session. By following these steps and guidelines, the Scrum team can ensure that the sprint review serves its intended purposes, gathering feedback and facilitating continuous improvement.

---

## Section 6.2: Conducting an Effective Sprint Review

The success of a sprint review not only depends on thorough preparation but also on the way it is conducted. This section discusses the key aspects of conducting an effective sprint review meeting.

### Meeting Location and Environment

Selecting an appropriate meeting location and creating the right environment are essential for a productive sprint review:

- **Physical or Virtual**: Determine whether the review will be conducted in a physical space or virtually, depending on team and stakeholder locations.

- **Comfortable Space**: Ensure the meeting space is comfortable, well-lit, and equipped with necessary technology for virtual meetings.

- **Engagement**: Create an engaging atmosphere that encourages open communication and collaboration.

### Agenda and Timebox

An agenda provides structure to the sprint review meeting:

- **Time Allocation**: Allocate specific time for each agenda item to prevent overruns.

- **Stick to the Agenda**: Adhere to the predefined agenda to maintain focus and prevent distractions.

### Product Demonstration

The heart of the sprint review is the product demonstration:

- **Hands-On**: Allow stakeholders to interact with the product increment whenever possible.

- **Narration**: Provide a narrative during the demonstration, explaining the features and how they align with user needs.

Engage stakeholders actively to make the review meaningful:

- **Feedback Collection**: Encourage stakeholders to provide constructive feedback on the product.

- **Question Handling**: Be prepared to address questions and concerns from attendees.



Transparency is a core Scrum value, and it's crucial during the sprint review:

- **Honesty**: Be honest about what was achieved and any challenges faced during the sprint.

- **Avoid Blame**: Focus on identifying improvements rather than assigning blame for any issues.



Acknowledge the team's hard work and accomplishments:

- **Recognize Efforts**: Celebrate milestones and achievements, fostering a positive team spirit.

- **Motivation**: Recognizing contributions boosts team motivation.



The sprint review should result in actionable items:

- **Identify Actions**: List action items and improvements that emerged from the review.

- **Assign Responsibilities**: Assign responsible individuals or teams to action items.



Ensure that action items and improvements are followed up on:

- **Track Progress**: Monitor the progress of action items during the next sprint and subsequent reviews.

- **Continuous Improvement**: Use the feedback and insights from previous reviews to drive continuous improvement.



Maintain records of the sprint review:

- **Meeting Minutes**: Document meeting minutes that include key points discussed, feedback received, and action items.

- **Accessibility**: Share meeting minutes with all stakeholders for transparency and reference.

Feedback Loop

The sprint review is not the end; it's part of an ongoing feedback loop:

- **Feedback Incorporation**: Use feedback from the review to refine the product backlog and prioritize work for future sprints.

- **Iterative Process**: Understand that each sprint review contributes to an iterative process of improvement.

Conclusion

Conducting an effective sprint review is crucial for harnessing the benefits of the Scrum framework. By carefully considering the meeting environment, agenda, product demonstration, stakeholder engagement, transparency, and follow-up, a Scrum team can ensure that their sprint reviews are not only productive but also contribute to the continuous improvement of their product and processes.

---

## Section 6.3: The Sprint Retrospective: A Tool for Continuous Improvement

In the Scrum framework, the sprint retrospective is an indispensable ceremony that takes place after the sprint review. Unlike the sprint review, which focuses on the product increment, the sprint retrospective is entirely dedicated to process improvement. It provides a structured opportunity for the Scrum team to reflect on the sprint and identify areas for enhancement.

### The Purpose of the Sprint Retrospective

The primary goal of the sprint retrospective is to promote continuous improvement. This ceremony serves several important purposes:

- **Reflection**: It allows the Scrum team to reflect on the sprint, acknowledging what went well and what could be improved.

- **Collaboration**: It encourages open and honest communication among team members, fostering collaboration and trust.

- **Actionable Insights**: The retrospective generates actionable insights and identifies areas where processes can be refined.

- **Empowerment**: Team members are empowered to take ownership of improvements, making them accountable for their work.

## Structuring the Sprint Retrospective

A well-structured sprint retrospective is essential for its effectiveness:

- **Timebox**: Like other Scrum ceremonies, the sprint retrospective has a timebox. Typically, for a two-week sprint, it lasts around 1 to 1.5 hours.

- **Facilitation**: The Scrum Master or a designated facilitator leads the retrospective, ensuring that it stays on track and maintains a positive atmosphere.

## Key Activities in the Sprint Retrospective

The sprint retrospective typically follows a three-phase structure:

1. **Setting the Stage**: In this phase, the team prepares for the retrospective. It includes activities such as selecting a retrospective technique, setting the stage by discussing the purpose, and establishing the ground rules for the meeting.

2. **Gathering Data**: The team collects data about the sprint. This may involve examining metrics, reviewing the sprint backlog, and discussing incidents or events that occurred during the sprint.

3. **Generating Insights and Deciding on Actions**: In this phase, the team analyzes the gathered data to identify areas for improvement. They discuss what went well and what could have been better. Then, they decide on specific actions to take in the next sprint.

## Retrospective Techniques

There are various retrospective techniques that teams can choose from, depending on their preferences and objectives. Some popular techniques include:

- **Start-Stop-Continue**: Team members identify what they should start doing, stop doing, and continue doing in the next sprint.

- **Mad, Sad, Glad**: Team members express what made them mad, sad, or glad during the sprint, leading to discussions on how to improve.

- **4Ls (Liked, Learned, Lacked, Longed for)**: The team shares what they liked, learned, lacked, and longed for in the sprint.

- **Sailboat or Speedboat**: A visual metaphor where the team identifies anchors (things holding them back) and wind (things propelling them forward).

## Actionable Takeaways

A successful sprint retrospective results in actionable takeaways:

- **Action Items**: The team decides on concrete actions that will lead to improvement. These actions should be specific, measurable, achievable, relevant, and time-bound (SMART).

- **Ownership**: Assign responsibilities for each action item to team members or roles.

## Conclusion

The sprint retrospective is a powerful tool for continuous improvement in Scrum. When conducted effectively, it enables teams to reflect, collaborate, and take ownership of their processes. By identifying areas for enhancement and implementing actionable improvements in each sprint, Scrum teams can become more efficient and deliver higher-quality products.

---

## Section 6.4: Gathering Feedback and Learning from It

The sprint retrospective is a valuable opportunity for Scrum teams to gather feedback and learn from it. In this section, we will explore the importance of feedback in the retrospective process and how teams can effectively collect and utilize feedback to drive continuous improvement.

### The Role of Feedback

Feedback is an essential component of the sprint retrospective for several reasons:

- **Insight Generation**: Feedback provides valuable insights into what worked well and what didn't during the sprint. It helps teams understand the root causes of issues and successes.

- **Enhanced Awareness**: It increases awareness among team members about their contributions and interactions, fostering a culture of accountability and collaboration.

- **Objective Assessment**: Feedback offers an objective assessment of the team's performance, often uncovering blind spots that team members might not have noticed.

### Collecting Feedback

Collecting feedback during the sprint retrospective involves multiple aspects:

- **Encourage Openness**: Create an environment where team members feel safe sharing their thoughts and experiences honestly.

- **Diverse Perspectives**: Seek feedback from all team members, including developers, the Scrum Master, and the product owner. Each role brings a unique perspective.

- **Positive and Negative Feedback**: Welcome both positive and negative feedback. Positive feedback reinforces behaviors that should be continued, while negative feedback highlights areas for improvement.

- **Anonymous Feedback**: Consider using anonymous feedback mechanisms if team members are hesitant to share openly. This can be particularly useful when discussing sensitive topics.

- **Feedback Sources**: Gather feedback from various sources, including team members, stakeholders, and end-users if applicable.

- **Feedback Channels**: Use different channels for collecting feedback, such as surveys, one-on-one interviews, or group discussions, depending on the team's preferences.

### Structured Feedback

To make feedback actionable, it should be structured and specific:

- **Use Templates**: Provide templates or forms that team members can use to structure their feedback. For example, a "What Went Well" and "What Could Be Improved" template can be effective.

- **Quantify When Possible**: Encourage team members to quantify their feedback. For instance, instead of saying, "Communication was poor," encourage them to specify instances or examples.

- **Identify Root Causes**: When discussing issues or challenges, encourage team members to go beyond surface-level problems and identify the root causes.

- **Link to Actions**: Connect feedback to potential actions or improvements that can be taken in the next sprint.

### Learning and Improvement

Feedback without action is ineffective. After gathering feedback, teams must take concrete steps toward improvement:

- **Action Planning**: Use feedback as the basis for action planning during the retrospective. Identify specific actions that address the feedback received.

- **Assign Responsibilities**: Assign ownership of action items to team members or roles, ensuring accountability.

- **Follow-Up**: Regularly follow up on the progress of action items and discuss them in subsequent retrospectives.

- **Iterative Process**: Understand that improvement is an iterative process. Each sprint retrospective should build on the previous one, with feedback continuously driving refinement.

Gathering feedback and learning from it is a fundamental aspect of the sprint retrospective. By creating an environment that encourages open and constructive feedback, structuring feedback for clarity and specificity, and taking actionable steps to address it, Scrum teams can harness the power of feedback to drive continuous improvement in their processes, collaboration, and product development.

---

## Section 6.5: Actionable Takeaways from Retrospectives

In the sprint retrospective, one of the primary objectives is to identify actionable takeaways that can lead to improvements in the upcoming sprint. This section delves into the importance of actionable takeaways and how Scrum teams can effectively generate and implement them.

### Why Actionable Takeaways Matter

Actionable takeaways are crucial because they bridge the gap between identifying issues and actually making improvements. They transform retrospective discussions into concrete actions that can lead to positive changes. Here's why they matter:

- **Drive Continuous Improvement**: Actionable takeaways are the catalyst for continuous improvement. They are the means by which teams evolve and enhance their processes over time.

- **Accountability**: Assigning ownership to specific team members or roles for each takeaway creates accountability. This ensures that someone is responsible for seeing the improvement through.

- **Tangible Outcomes**: Actionable takeaways result in tangible outcomes that can be measured and assessed for their impact on the team's performance.

### Generating Actionable Takeaways

To generate meaningful and actionable takeaways from the sprint retrospective, consider the following best practices:

- **Specificity**: Make takeaways as specific as possible. Avoid vague statements and focus on precisely what needs to change or be improved.

- **Prioritization**: Not all issues identified during the retrospective will have equal importance. Prioritize takeaways based on their potential impact and feasibility.

- **SMART Goals**: Follow the SMART (Specific, Measurable, Achievable, Relevant, Time-bound) criteria when defining takeaways. This ensures they are well-defined and achievable.

- **Root Cause Analysis**: Dive deep into the root causes of issues or challenges. Addressing root causes is more effective than merely treating symptoms.

- **Use Data**: Whenever possible, support takeaways with data or evidence. Data-driven decisions are more compelling.



Identifying actionable takeaways is just the beginning. Implementing them effectively is equally important:

- **Ownership**: Assign clear ownership of each takeaway to a team member or role. This person is responsible for ensuring that the action is carried out.

- **Timeline**: Set a timeline or timeframe for implementing each takeaway. This adds a sense of urgency and prevents indefinite postponement.

- **Regular Updates**: Regularly review the status of each takeaway. Discuss progress, obstacles, and any adjustments needed during subsequent retrospectives.

- **Feedback Loop**: Encourage feedback from team members during the implementation process. Their insights can help refine actions and prevent potential roadblocks.

- **Celebrate Successes**: When a takeaway leads to a positive change or improvement, celebrate it with the team. Recognizing successes reinforces the importance of the retrospective process.



Actionable takeaways are not just a one-time activity; they are part of fostering a culture of continuous improvement within a Scrum team. The process of identifying, implementing, and evaluating takeaways should be ongoing, with each sprint retrospective building on the previous one.

By consistently generating and acting upon actionable takeaways, Scrum teams can streamline their processes, enhance collaboration, and deliver higher-quality products. This iterative approach to improvement is at the core of Scrum's effectiveness in adapting to change and delivering value to stakeholders.

# Chapter 7: Scaling Scrum Across the Organization

## Section 7.1: When and How to Scale

Scaling Scrum is a natural progression for organizations that have experienced the benefits of Agile and Scrum at the team level and now seek to expand those benefits throughout the entire organization. In this section, we will explore the key considerations for determining when and how to scale Scrum.

### Understanding the Need for Scaling

Before embarking on the journey of scaling Scrum, it's essential to identify the need for it. Several indicators suggest that an organization might benefit from scaling:

- **Complexity**: When projects or products become too complex for a single Scrum team to handle, it's a sign that scaling may be necessary.

- **Multiple Teams**: If an organization has multiple Scrum teams working on interrelated components or products, coordinating their efforts can be challenging without a scaling framework.

- **Global Reach**: Organizations with distributed teams across different geographical locations may require scaling to ensure efficient collaboration.

- **Increasing Demand**: A surge in demand for Agile practices across various departments or business units is an indicator that scaling may be advantageous.

- **Alignment**: When an organization seeks better alignment between its strategic objectives and the work being done by Agile teams, scaling can help achieve that alignment.

### Choosing a Scaling Framework

Once the need for scaling is recognized, the next step is to choose an appropriate scaling framework. Several frameworks are available, each with its principles, practices, and guidelines. Common scaling frameworks include:

- **SAFe (Scaled Agile Framework)**: SAFe is one of the most widely adopted scaling frameworks. It provides a comprehensive set of roles, events, and artifacts to scale Agile across large organizations.

- **LeSS (Large Scale Scrum)**: LeSS is an approach to scaling Scrum by simplifying it. It emphasizes transparency, empiricism, and lean thinking.

- **Nexus**: Nexus is a framework specifically designed for scaling Scrum. It builds on the principles of Scrum and offers additional practices for managing dependencies among multiple Scrum teams.

- **Scrum@Scale**: Developed by the co-creator of Scrum, Scrum@Scale is designed to extend Scrum's benefits throughout an entire organization.



Scaling Scrum involves more than simply applying a framework. It requires a cultural shift, organizational support, and careful planning:

- **Leadership Buy-In**: Executives and leaders must be aligned with the decision to scale and provide active support.

- **Training and Education**: Team members and leaders need training to understand the chosen framework and its principles.

- **Clear Objectives**: Define clear objectives and outcomes for scaling. What does success look like, and what are the key performance indicators?

- **Pilot Phase**: Consider starting with a pilot project or team to test the chosen scaling framework before rolling it out organization-wide.

- **Continuous Improvement**: Just like in Scrum at the team level, scaling Scrum requires a commitment to continuous improvement. Regular retrospectives and adjustments are crucial.



Scaling Scrum can be a powerful way to extend the benefits of Agile and Scrum principles throughout an organization. However, it's not a one-size-fits-all solution. Organizations must carefully assess their needs, choose an appropriate framework, and prepare for the cultural and structural changes that scaling entails. When done effectively, scaling Scrum can lead to improved collaboration, faster delivery of value, and better alignment with strategic goals.

---

## Section 7.2: Frameworks for Scaling Scrum: SAFe, LeSS, and Others

Scaling Scrum requires a well-defined framework that provides structure and guidelines for coordinating the work of multiple Scrum teams. In this section, we will explore some of the popular frameworks for scaling Scrum, including SAFe (Scaled Agile Framework), LeSS (Large Scale Scrum), and a few others.

### SAFe (Scaled Agile Framework)

**SAFe**, the Scaled Agile Framework, is one of the most widely adopted frameworks for scaling Scrum and Agile practices in large organizations. SAFe provides a comprehensive set of roles, events, and artifacts that help coordinate the work of multiple Agile teams. Some key components of SAFe include:

- **Release Trains**: SAFe organizes teams into "Release Trains," which are groups of Agile teams that work together to deliver value to the customer. Each Release Train has a defined Program Backlog and a set of Program Increment (PI) objectives.

- **PI Planning**: SAFe's Program Increment (PI) Planning is a significant event where teams come together to plan and commit to delivering a set of features and stories over a fixed time frame, typically 8-12 weeks.

- **Roles**: SAFe defines several roles, including Release Train Engineer (RTE), Product Owner, Scrum Master, and System Architect, among others, to support coordination and alignment.

- **Principles**: SAFe is based on a set of Lean-Agile principles that guide decision-making and behavior at all levels of the organization.

## LeSS (Large Scale Scrum)

**LeSS**, or Large Scale Scrum, takes a different approach to scaling Scrum. It simplifies the Scrum framework and retains its core principles of transparency, inspection, and adaptation. Key aspects of LeSS include:

- **One Scrum**: LeSS operates under the philosophy of "One Scrum," meaning that it treats the entire organization as a single Scrum Team, rather than dividing it into separate teams or layers.

- **Minimal Artifacts**: LeSS reduces the number of roles and artifacts, emphasizing the importance of a single Product Owner, one Product Backlog, and one Definition of Done for all teams.

- **Organizational Design**: LeSS encourages organizations to rethink their structure, reduce hierarchy, and minimize dependencies to enhance the agility of the entire organization.

## Nexus

**Nexus** is a scaling framework specifically designed to extend Scrum principles and practices for larger and more complex product development efforts. Key features of Nexus include:

- **Nexus Integration Team**: Nexus introduces the role of a Nexus Integration Team, responsible for coordinating and integrating the work of multiple Scrum Teams.

- **Nexus Events**: Nexus includes additional events such as the Nexus Sprint Review and Nexus Sprint Retrospective to facilitate coordination and alignment among teams.

- **Nexus+**: Nexus+ is an extension of Nexus that addresses even larger and more complex scaling challenges.

**Scrum@Scale**, created by Jeff Sutherland, one of the co-creators of Scrum, is designed to scale Scrum across the entire organization. It emphasizes the importance of Scrum at every level, from individual teams to the executive leadership. Key aspects of Scrum@Scale include:

- **Scale-Free Architecture**: Scrum@Scale introduces a scale-free architecture, which allows organizations to scale Scrum without adding unnecessary complexity.

- **Scrum of Scrums**: Scrum@Scale uses a Scrum of Scrums approach to coordinate the work of multiple teams. Each team operates as a Scrum Team and interacts with other teams through the Scrum of Scrums.

- **Executive Action Teams**: Scrum@Scale involves creating Executive Action Teams (EATs) to align the organization's strategic goals with the work of Agile teams.

These are just a few of the popular frameworks for scaling Scrum. Each framework has its own strengths and suitability for different organizational contexts. Choosing the right framework requires careful consideration of the organization's goals, culture, and specific scaling challenges. Ultimately, the goal of any scaling framework is to enable organizations to deliver value more effectively while maintaining the core principles of Agile and Scrum.

---

## Section 7.3: The Scrum Master's Role in Scaling

Scaling Scrum within an organization is a complex endeavor that involves various stakeholders and requires careful coordination. The role of the Scrum Master, a pivotal figure in Scrum, also evolves when scaling Scrum to ensure the framework's success at a larger scale. In this section, we'll explore the Scrum Master's role in scaling Scrum and how it differs from their traditional responsibilities within a single Scrum Team.

### Understanding the Expanding Scope

When an organization scales Scrum, it typically involves multiple Scrum Teams working on interconnected projects or products. The Scrum Master's role expands to support these teams and address challenges that arise due to the increased complexity. Here are key aspects of the Scrum Master's evolving role in scaling Scrum:

1. **Team of Scrum Masters**: In a scaled Scrum environment, there may be a team of Scrum Masters, each responsible for one or more Scrum Teams. These Scrum Masters collaborate to ensure alignment, share best practices, and tackle cross-team impediments.

2. **Facilitator of Scrum Events**: The Scrum Master continues to facilitate Scrum events such as Sprint Planning, Daily Stand-ups, Sprint Reviews, and Sprint

Retrospectives. However, they now work to synchronize these events across multiple teams and ensure that dependencies are managed effectively.

3. **Scaling Agile Practices**: The Scrum Master helps in scaling Agile practices, ensuring that teams adopt consistent processes and workflows. They assist in creating a standard set of practices and guidelines that work across teams.

4. **Removing Cross-Team Impediments**: With multiple teams collaborating, cross-team impediments become more common. The Scrum Master plays a crucial role in identifying and eliminating these impediments, whether they are related to resource allocation, dependencies, or conflicting priorities.

5. **Coaching and Mentoring**: The Scrum Master continues to coach and mentor Scrum Teams, Product Owners, and stakeholders. They also support other Scrum Masters in their coaching efforts to maintain a high level of Agile maturity across the organization.

6. **Facilitating Collaboration**: Collaboration between teams is vital in scaling Scrum. Scrum Masters facilitate communication, collaboration, and knowledge sharing among teams to ensure a seamless flow of information and alignment of goals.

7. **Supporting Product Owners**: The Scrum Master assists Product Owners in managing large Product Backlogs, setting priorities, and ensuring that the product vision is understood and followed by all teams.

## Challenges and Adaptation

Scaling Scrum presents unique challenges that Scrum Masters must address:

- **Increased Complexity**: Dealing with multiple teams, dependencies, and larger-scale planning introduces complexity that Scrum Masters need to manage effectively.

- **Alignment**: Ensuring that all teams are aligned with the organization's objectives and working towards a common goal can be challenging.

- **Coaching at Scale**: Coaching and mentoring multiple teams simultaneously requires advanced coaching skills and time management.

- **Overcoming Resistance**: Resistance to change can be more pronounced in larger organizations. Scrum Masters need to navigate resistance and foster an Agile mindset.

In conclusion, the Scrum Master's role in scaling Scrum is critical for the successful adoption of Agile practices across an organization. They become champions of Agile values and principles, working to ensure that the organization can deliver value efficiently and effectively in a scaled environment. Adaptation, collaboration, and a deep understanding of Agile principles are essential for Scrum Masters as they take on this expanded role.

Scaling Scrum can bring numerous benefits, but it also comes with its fair share of challenges. Understanding these challenges and having strategies to overcome them is crucial for a successful implementation. In this section, we will delve into some common challenges faced when scaling Scrum and explore strategies to address them.

### Challenge 1: Coordination and Communication

In a large-scale Scrum setup, with multiple teams working on interrelated projects or products, coordination and communication become complex. Teams may struggle to share information effectively, leading to misunderstandings and delays.

**Solution**: Implement a well-defined communication plan that includes regular cross-team meetings, shared collaboration tools, and a clear structure for reporting and sharing information. Use Agile practices like Daily Scrum of Scrums to improve coordination.

### Challenge 2: Scaling Agile Roles

Scaling Scrum often means having more Product Owners and Scrum Masters. Finding qualified individuals for these roles can be challenging, and aligning them with the organization's vision can be even harder.

**Solution**: Invest in training and certification programs for Scrum Masters and Product Owners. Foster a culture of continuous learning and promote internal talent development. Ensure that all Product Owners share a common vision and collaborate effectively.

### Challenge 3: Maintaining Consistency

Maintaining consistency in processes and practices across multiple teams is a significant challenge. Teams may interpret Scrum differently, leading to misalignment.

**Solution**: Develop and document a set of standard practices and guidelines that all teams must follow. Conduct regular reviews and inspections to ensure compliance and address discrepancies promptly.

### Challenge 4: Dependency Management

As the number of teams increases, so do dependencies between them. Managing dependencies can become a bottleneck if not handled effectively.

**Solution**: Identify and visualize dependencies using tools like Dependency Boards. Encourage teams to work collaboratively to resolve dependencies and adopt practices like feature flags to decouple releases.

Resistance to Agile practices and scaling Scrum can come from various quarters within the organization, including team members, middle management, and executives.

**Solution**: Provide extensive training and coaching to all stakeholders. Communicate the benefits of Agile practices and scaling Scrum clearly, addressing concerns and misconceptions. Show early successes to build confidence in the new approach.



Scaling Scrum often necessitates a shift in the role of the Scrum Master from focusing solely on one team to overseeing multiple teams. This shift can be challenging for Scrum Masters.

**Solution**: Invest in Scrum Master training and development programs that focus on the skills required for scaling Scrum. Encourage Scrum Masters to collaborate and share experiences with each other. Create a mentorship program for newer Scrum Masters.



Conducting effective retrospectives in a scaled Scrum environment can be challenging due to the larger number of participants and diverse teams.

**Solution**: Consider dividing retrospectives into team-level and cross-team retrospectives. Use techniques like Lean Coffee or online collaboration tools to facilitate retrospectives effectively.



Scaling Scrum is not just about following processes; it's about embracing an Agile mindset throughout the organization. Without this mindset shift, the benefits of scaling Scrum may not fully materialize.

**Solution**: Invest in Agile culture-building initiatives. Encourage leadership to lead by example and exhibit Agile values. Celebrate Agile successes and promote a culture of continuous improvement.

In conclusion, scaling Scrum is a complex journey that requires careful planning, commitment, and adaptability. By acknowledging these challenges and proactively implementing solutions, organizations can successfully scale Scrum and realize the benefits of Agile practices at a larger scale.

---

## Section 7.5: Case Studies: Successful Scrum Scaling

In this section, we will explore real-world case studies of organizations that successfully scaled Scrum to address complex challenges and achieve significant improvements in their development processes.

**Background**: Spotify, a global music streaming service, faced challenges in coordinating development efforts across multiple teams. They adopted a model called "Spotify Model" or "Spotify Squad Framework" to scale Scrum successfully.

**Approach**: Spotify organized its engineering teams into cross-functional squads, each responsible for specific features or parts of the product. Squads were autonomous and followed Agile practices like Scrum and Kanban. Squads were grouped into "tribes" based on related functions, and chapters and guilds were established to promote knowledge sharing and collaboration.

**Outcome**: The Spotify Model allowed for efficient scaling while maintaining agility. Squads could work independently while aligning with the organization's strategic goals. This approach encouraged innovation, improved communication, and enabled the rapid development of new features.



**Background**: Intel, a leading technology company, faced the challenge of coordinating and scaling Agile practices across its global teams. They adopted the Scaled Agile Framework (SAFe) to address these challenges.

**Approach**: Intel implemented SAFe, a comprehensive framework for scaling Agile and Lean practices. SAFe provided a structured approach to scaling Scrum, including roles like Release Trains, Solution Trains, and Lean-Agile principles. It emphasized alignment, collaboration, and delivery.

**Outcome**: SAFe enabled Intel to coordinate efforts across teams, improve product quality, and accelerate time-to-market. It provided a common language and framework that facilitated communication and alignment at scale.



**Background**: ING Bank, a global financial institution, wanted to transform its IT department to be more Agile and customer-focused. They adopted the "ING Agile Way of Working" to scale Scrum and Agile practices.

**Approach**: ING introduced the "ING Agile Way of Working," which combined Scrum, Kanban, and Lean principles. They organized teams into "tribes," "squads," "chapters," and "guilds," similar to the Spotify Model. ING also focused on continuous improvement and the development of an Agile mindset.

**Outcome**: ING Bank saw improved customer satisfaction, faster delivery of features, and increased employee engagement. The new way of working encouraged collaboration, reduced dependencies, and allowed teams to respond more effectively to changing market conditions.

**Background**: Salesforce, a global leader in customer relationship management (CRM) software, needed to scale its Agile practices to keep pace with rapid growth. They adopted a customized approach to scale Scrum.

**Approach**: Salesforce introduced the "Agile Release Train" (ART) concept, where multiple Agile teams collaboratively delivered value. They established a regular PI (Program Increment) planning event to align teams and prioritize work. The ART was part of the larger SAFe framework but tailored to their needs.

**Outcome**: Salesforce achieved faster delivery, improved collaboration between teams, and better visibility into project status. The ART approach allowed them to respond to market demands more efficiently and ensure customer satisfaction.

These case studies highlight that successful scaling of Scrum is achievable through various approaches tailored to the organization's specific context. By adopting frameworks like SAFe or customizing their Agile models, organizations can effectively address scalability challenges and reap the benefits of Agile principles at a larger scale.

# Chapter 8: Advanced Scrum Master Skills

## Section 8.1: Coaching and Mentoring Techniques

In this section, we will delve into the essential skills and techniques that a Scrum Master needs to effectively coach and mentor Agile teams. Coaching and mentoring are critical aspects of the Scrum Master's role, as they help teams continuously improve and achieve higher levels of performance.

### The Role of a Scrum Master as a Coach

A Scrum Master is often compared to a coach or a guide who helps the team navigate the challenges of Agile development. Here are some key aspects of a Scrum Master's role as a coach:

1. **Facilitating Self-Organization**: A Scrum Master encourages teams to become self-organizing by providing guidance rather than direct instructions. This empowerment fosters a sense of ownership and responsibility among team members.

2. **Active Listening**: Effective coaching begins with active listening. Scrum Masters should listen to team members' concerns, challenges, and ideas attentively. This not only builds trust but also helps in understanding the team's needs.

3. **Asking Powerful Questions**: Asking open-ended and thought-provoking questions can stimulate critical thinking within the team. Scrum Masters use questions to help teams reflect on their processes and identify areas for improvement.

4. **Feedback and Reflection**: Continuous feedback is crucial for improvement. Scrum Masters facilitate feedback sessions, retrospectives, and reviews to help the team reflect on their work and identify opportunities for growth.

### Coaching Models and Approaches

To be an effective coach, Scrum Masters often leverage various coaching models and approaches. Some commonly used coaching models include:

*1. GROW Model:*
- **Goals**: Coaches help individuals or teams define clear goals.
- **Reality**: Understanding the current reality and challenges.
- **Options**: Exploring possible options and strategies.
- **Will**: Commitment to taking action and achieving the goals.

*2. Socratic Questioning:*
- Using open-ended questions to encourage critical thinking and problem-solving.

- Applying Kanban principles to coaching, visualizing work, limiting work in progress, and focusing on flow.

## Mentoring vs. Coaching

While coaching and mentoring share similarities, they have distinct differences:

- **Coaching**: Focuses on helping individuals or teams find their own solutions and make decisions. Coaches ask questions and facilitate self-discovery.

- **Mentoring**: Involves sharing knowledge and experiences with the mentee. Mentors provide guidance based on their expertise and past experiences.

Scrum Masters often balance between coaching and mentoring based on the team's needs and the situation at hand.

## Challenges in Coaching

Coaching is not always straightforward, and Scrum Masters may encounter various challenges:

- **Resistance to Change**: Some team members may resist coaching, as it involves change and self-reflection. Building trust is crucial to overcome this resistance.

- **Time Constraints**: Scrum Masters may have limited time for coaching due to other responsibilities. Effective time management is essential.

- **Cultural Differences**: In multicultural teams, understanding and respecting diverse cultural backgrounds is vital for successful coaching.

## Continuous Improvement as a Coach

A Scrum Master's coaching skills should continually evolve. They can achieve this by:

- Seeking feedback from teams and peers.
- Participating in coaching communities and training.
- Reading books and articles on coaching and Agile practices.

In conclusion, coaching and mentoring are integral components of a Scrum Master's role. Effective coaching empowers teams to self-organize, reflect on their practices, and continuously improve. Scrum Masters should adopt various coaching models, listen actively, and balance coaching and mentoring to meet the team's specific needs. Overcoming challenges and committing to continuous improvement as a coach are essential aspects of mastering this skill.

In Agile teams, conflicts are inevitable due to the dynamic nature of the work and the collaboration required. Scrum Masters need to be skilled in conflict resolution to maintain a healthy team environment and facilitate productive discussions. This section explores advanced conflict resolution strategies that Scrum Masters can employ.

## Understanding Conflict in Agile Teams

Conflict can arise for various reasons in Agile teams, including differences in opinions, misunderstandings, competition for resources, and stress from tight deadlines. However, not all conflicts are negative; some can lead to innovation and better solutions. It's essential for Scrum Masters to differentiate between healthy and harmful conflicts.

## Conflict Resolution Styles

Scrum Masters should be aware of different conflict resolution styles and when to apply them:

1. **Collaboration**: Encouraging open communication and problem-solving among team members. This approach is effective for complex issues that require multiple perspectives.

2. **Compromise**: Finding a middle ground when parties have conflicting interests. Scrum Masters can facilitate compromise by helping teams identify what they can give up without compromising their core objectives.

3. **Avoidance**: Sometimes, it's best to avoid conflicts that aren't crucial to the project's success. However, continuous avoidance can lead to unresolved issues, so Scrum Masters should use this approach sparingly.

4. **Accommodation**: Prioritizing the needs and concerns of others over personal interests. This style can help maintain relationships within the team but may not always be appropriate.

5. **Competing**: Asserting one's viewpoint and pursuing personal goals at the expense of others. Scrum Masters should use this approach carefully, as it can damage relationships.

## Advanced Conflict Resolution Techniques

In addition to the basic conflict resolution styles, Scrum Masters can employ advanced techniques:

### 1. Root Cause Analysis:

- Identifying the underlying causes of conflicts rather than addressing symptoms. Scrum Masters can facilitate root cause analysis sessions to get to the core issues.

**2. Negotiation Skills:**

- Developing negotiation skills to help parties come to a mutually beneficial agreement. Scrum Masters should act as neutral facilitators during negotiations.

**3. Mediation:**

- Serving as a mediator when conflicts involve multiple parties. Scrum Masters can help mediate discussions and find common ground.

**4. Facilitation:**

- Skilled facilitation of team discussions and meetings to ensure that all voices are heard and that conflicts are addressed constructively.

## Conflict Resolution Frameworks

There are several conflict resolution frameworks that Scrum Masters can follow:

**1. The Thomas-Kilmann Conflict Mode Instrument:**

- This model assesses an individual's tendency to use five conflict resolution styles: competing, collaborating, compromising, avoiding, and accommodating. Scrum Masters can use this tool to understand team members' preferences and encourage appropriate styles.

**2. The Conflict Resolution Onion:**

- This model suggests that conflicts have multiple layers, ranging from surface-level issues to deep-seated values and beliefs. Scrum Masters can use this framework to peel away the layers and address the core causes of conflicts.

## Common Challenges in Conflict Resolution

Scrum Masters may encounter challenges in resolving conflicts, such as:

- **Lack of Trust**: Teams with low trust levels may struggle to openly discuss conflicts. Building trust is essential for effective conflict resolution.

- **Emotional Escalation**: Emotions can run high during conflicts. Scrum Masters should be skilled in managing emotional situations and keeping discussions constructive.

- **Power Imbalance**: Imbalances in power can affect conflict resolution. Scrum Masters must ensure that all team members have an equal voice.

## Continuous Improvement in Conflict Resolution

To enhance their conflict resolution skills, Scrum Masters should:

- Seek feedback from team members and stakeholders.
- Participate in conflict resolution workshops and training.
- Read books and articles on conflict resolution and mediation techniques.

In conclusion, advanced conflict resolution is a critical skill for Scrum Masters. By understanding the nature of conflicts, using appropriate resolution styles and techniques, and applying conflict resolution frameworks, Scrum Masters can help teams navigate challenges effectively and maintain a positive working environment. Continuous improvement in conflict resolution is essential for becoming a skilled Scrum Master.

---

## Section 8.3: Fostering High-Performance Teams

One of the primary responsibilities of a Scrum Master is to foster high-performance teams that can consistently deliver value to the organization. In this section, we will explore strategies and techniques for achieving and maintaining high-performance within Agile teams.

### The Importance of High-Performance Teams

High-performance teams are the backbone of Agile development. They are more likely to meet sprint goals, adapt to changes quickly, and produce high-quality work. Such teams are also more engaged and satisfied with their work, which contributes to reduced turnover and increased productivity. Here are some key aspects to consider when fostering high-performance teams:

### 1. Clear Goals and Objectives

High-performance teams have a shared understanding of their goals and objectives. The Scrum Master plays a crucial role in ensuring that the team understands the sprint goals, product vision, and the value they are expected to deliver. This clarity helps team members align their efforts and work towards a common purpose.

### 2. Empowered and Autonomous

High-performance teams are empowered to make decisions and take ownership of their work. Scrum Masters should facilitate an environment where team members have the autonomy to make choices about how they will meet their commitments. This empowerment increases accountability and motivation.

### 3. Effective Collaboration

Collaboration is at the core of Agile methodologies. Scrum Masters should encourage open communication and collaboration within the team. Techniques like daily stand-up meetings, pair programming, and regular retrospectives help build a culture of collaboration and continuous improvement.

### 4. Continuous Learning

High-performance teams are committed to continuous learning and self-improvement. Scrum Masters should support team members in acquiring new skills and knowledge. This can involve providing training opportunities, sharing best practices, and encouraging experimentation.



Agile teams need to be adaptable to respond to changing requirements and market conditions. Scrum Masters should foster a mindset of adaptability and help the team embrace change as an opportunity for improvement.

## Strategies for Fostering High-Performance Teams

Here are some strategies that Scrum Masters can employ to foster high-performance teams:

### 1. Lead by Example

Scrum Masters should lead by example, demonstrating the values and principles of Agile methodologies. Their actions and behaviors set the tone for the team.

### 2. Remove Impediments

Scrum Masters should actively identify and remove impediments that hinder the team's progress. This could involve addressing technical issues, resolving conflicts, or ensuring access to necessary resources.

### 3. Provide Continuous Feedback

Regular feedback is essential for improvement. Scrum Masters should provide constructive feedback to individual team members and the team as a whole. Feedback should be specific, timely, and focused on improvement.

### 4. Celebrate Achievements

Recognizing and celebrating achievements, both big and small, boosts team morale and motivation. Scrum Masters should acknowledge and celebrate the team's successes to reinforce positive behaviors.

### 5. Coach and Mentor

Scrum Masters should coach and mentor team members, helping them grow both professionally and personally. This involves providing guidance, facilitating skill development, and offering support.

### 6. Foster a Safe Environment

High-performance teams thrive in a psychologically safe environment where team members feel comfortable expressing their ideas, asking questions, and taking risks. Scrum Masters should create and maintain this safe space.

Scrum Masters should continuously monitor the health of the team by tracking key metrics, conducting retrospectives, and gauging team morale. Addressing issues promptly prevents them from escalating.

### Challenges in Fostering High-Performance

While fostering high-performance teams is essential, it comes with its challenges. Some common challenges include:

- **Resistance to Change**: Team members may resist changes in processes or practices. Scrum Masters need to effectively manage this resistance and communicate the benefits of change.

- **Conflict and Personality Clashes**: Conflicts can arise within teams, affecting performance. Scrum Masters should employ conflict resolution techniques to address these issues.

- **Burnout**: Overworking and burnout can lead to decreased performance. Scrum Masters should be vigilant about team members' workloads and well-being.

- **Lack of Resources**: Teams may struggle if they lack necessary resources or tools. Scrum Masters should advocate for the team's needs and work with stakeholders to secure resources.

In conclusion, fostering high-performance teams is a key responsibility of a Scrum Master. It involves creating an environment of clarity, empowerment, collaboration, and continuous improvement. Scrum Masters should employ various strategies to support the team in achieving and maintaining high levels of performance while addressing challenges that may arise along the way.

---

## Section 8.4: Navigating Organizational Politics

Organizational politics is an inevitable aspect of working in any large organization. It involves the use of power, influence, and networks to achieve personal or departmental objectives. As a Scrum Master, navigating organizational politics is essential to create an environment conducive to Agile practices and high-performance teams. In this section, we will explore strategies for effectively dealing with organizational politics and maintaining the integrity of Scrum.

### The Impact of Organizational Politics

Organizational politics can have both positive and negative impacts on Agile teams and their ability to deliver value. Understanding these impacts is crucial:

1. **Resource Allocation**: Effective navigation of politics can help secure the necessary resources and support for Agile initiatives, such as training, tools, or additional team members.

2. **Stakeholder Engagement**: Building relationships with influential stakeholders can lead to their active support of Agile practices, which can facilitate smoother project execution.

3. **Advocacy for Agile**: Skilled Scrum Masters can advocate for Agile principles and practices within the organization, helping to create a culture that values Agile approaches.



1. **Misalignment with Agile Values**: Organizational politics can sometimes push teams and individuals toward behaviors that contradict Agile values and principles, such as transparency and collaboration.

2. **Resource Constraints**: Politics may lead to resource constraints or allocation decisions that hinder Agile teams' ability to deliver value.

3. **Resistance to Change**: Political resistance to change can manifest as opposition to Agile transformations or reluctance to adopt Agile practices.

## Strategies for Navigating Organizational Politics

As a Scrum Master, you play a pivotal role in mitigating the negative impacts of organizational politics while leveraging its positive aspects. Here are strategies to help you navigate organizational politics effectively:

### 1. Build Relationships

Develop strong relationships with key stakeholders, including managers, department heads, and influential individuals. Understand their perspectives and concerns to bridge the gap between organizational politics and Agile values.

### 2. Be Transparent

Maintain transparency in your actions and communication. Clearly communicate the benefits of Agile practices to stakeholders, emphasizing how they align with organizational goals and objectives.

### 3. Educate and Advocate

Educate stakeholders about Agile methodologies and their advantages. Advocate for Agile practices by showcasing their success stories and quantifiable benefits within the organization.

*4. Align with Organizational Goals*

Ensure that Agile initiatives and team goals align with the broader organizational objectives. This alignment can help secure support from senior leadership.

*5. Anticipate and Address Resistance*

Proactively identify potential sources of resistance to Agile practices. Address concerns and misconceptions by providing evidence, conducting workshops, or involving resistant individuals in Agile events.

*6. Collaborate with Change Agents*

Identify change agents within the organization who can help influence decisions in favor of Agile. Collaborate with them to drive Agile transformations and overcome political barriers.

*7. Use Data and Metrics*

Leverage data and metrics to demonstrate the positive impact of Agile practices. Metrics such as velocity, lead time, and customer satisfaction can provide compelling evidence of Agile's effectiveness.

*8. Stay Neutral*

Maintain a neutral stance in political discussions and conflicts. Focus on facilitating collaboration and achieving project goals rather than taking sides.

*9. Seek Support from Agile Communities*

Connect with Agile communities and networks outside your organization. Sharing experiences and seeking advice from the broader Agile community can provide valuable insights and support.

*10. Promote a Culture of Continuous Improvement*

Encourage a culture of continuous improvement within your team and organization. Emphasize the importance of learning from mistakes and adapting to change.

### Challenges in Navigating Organizational Politics

While these strategies can be effective, Scrum Masters may encounter various challenges when dealing with organizational politics:

- **Lack of Awareness**: Some stakeholders may not fully understand Agile principles, making it challenging to gain their support.

- **Competing Interests**: Different departments and individuals may have conflicting interests, leading to political conflicts.

- **Resistance from Hierarchies**: Organizational hierarchies and established power structures may resist Agile transformations.

- **Short-Term vs. Long-Term Goals**: Some stakeholders may prioritize short-term goals over long-term Agile benefits.

In conclusion, organizational politics is a complex and unavoidable aspect of working in large organizations. Scrum Masters must learn to navigate it effectively to support Agile initiatives and maintain the integrity of Scrum. Building relationships, staying transparent, advocating for Agile, and aligning with organizational goals are key strategies to overcome challenges and foster an Agile-friendly environment.

---

## Section 8.5: Continuous Learning and Self-Improvement

Continuous learning and self-improvement are essential aspects of a Scrum Master's role. In the dynamic and evolving world of Agile and Scrum, staying up-to-date with the latest practices, tools, and techniques is crucial for success. This section explores the significance of continuous learning, various ways to enhance your skills, and the benefits it brings to your role as a Scrum Master.

### The Importance of Continuous Learning

The field of Agile and Scrum is constantly evolving. New methodologies, tools, and best practices emerge regularly. As a Scrum Master, embracing continuous learning offers several advantages:

*1. Staying Relevant:*

To effectively guide Agile teams, you must stay current with the latest Agile frameworks, techniques, and industry trends. Continuous learning ensures you remain relevant in a rapidly changing landscape.

*2. Adapting to Change:*

Agile principles emphasize adaptability and responding to change. Continuous learning equips you with the knowledge and skills needed to adapt to evolving project requirements and challenges.

*3. Enhancing Problem-Solving:*

Learning from diverse sources and experiences broadens your problem-solving abilities. You can apply insights from various domains to address complex issues within your Scrum teams.

Continuous learning enables you to bring additional value to your teams by introducing new tools, techniques, and strategies that can improve processes and outcomes.

## Ways to Facilitate Continuous Learning

To foster continuous learning and self-improvement as a Scrum Master, consider the following approaches:

*1. Attend Training and Workshops:*

Participate in Agile and Scrum training courses, workshops, and certifications. These structured learning opportunities provide a solid foundation and help you stay updated on best practices.

*2. Read Agile Literature:*

Explore Agile and Scrum literature, books, articles, and blogs written by experts in the field. Reading exposes you to different perspectives and innovative ideas.

*3. Join Agile Communities:*

Engage with Agile communities, forums, and user groups. Networking with other Scrum Masters and Agile enthusiasts allows you to share experiences, ask questions, and learn from others.

*4. Mentoring and Coaching:*

Seek mentorship or coaching from experienced Agile practitioners. Learning from someone with more experience can accelerate your growth as a Scrum Master.

*5. Reflect and Experiment:*

Regularly reflect on your own experiences and experiment with new practices within your teams. This hands-on learning can lead to valuable insights.

*6. Attend Conferences:*

Attend Agile and Scrum conferences and events. These gatherings provide opportunities to hear from industry leaders, participate in workshops, and gain exposure to cutting-edge practices.

*7. Online Courses and Webinars:*

Enroll in online courses and webinars on Agile and Scrum topics. These platforms offer flexibility in learning and often include interactive elements.

Consider training in related areas, such as leadership, communication, or conflict resolution. These skills are invaluable in your role as a Scrum Master.

*9. Peer Learning:*

Collaborate with other Scrum Masters and colleagues to exchange knowledge and insights. Peer learning can lead to innovative solutions and best practices.

## Measuring the Impact of Continuous Learning

Evaluating the impact of continuous learning is essential to ensure that your efforts are contributing to your effectiveness as a Scrum Master. Consider the following metrics:

*1. Team Performance Metrics:*

Monitor key performance indicators (KPIs) related to your Scrum teams, such as velocity, sprint success rate, and customer satisfaction. Improvements in these metrics may indicate the positive impact of your continuous learning efforts.

*2. Feedback from Teams:*

Solicit feedback from your Scrum teams about your performance as a Scrum Master. Their insights can help you identify areas where your learning efforts have made a difference.

*3. Successful Agile Adoption:*

Evaluate the successful adoption of Agile principles and practices within your organization. Assess whether your continuous learning initiatives have contributed to this success.

*4. Personal Growth:*

Reflect on your personal growth and development as a Scrum Master. Consider how your skills, knowledge, and abilities have evolved over time.

In conclusion, continuous learning and self-improvement are integral to your role as a Scrum Master. Embrace a proactive approach to learning, leverage various resources and opportunities, and measure the impact of your efforts. By continuously enhancing your knowledge and skills, you can better support your Scrum teams and contribute to the success of Agile initiatives within your organization.

# Chapter 9: Scrum in Different Industry Contexts

In this chapter, we will explore how Scrum, a framework originally developed for software development, has found applications in various industries beyond IT. Scrum's principles of collaboration, adaptability, and iterative progress make it adaptable to diverse domains. Section 9.1 dives into the realm of software development, highlighting how Scrum has been applied effectively in this context.

## Section 9.1: Scrum in Software Development

Software development was the birthplace of Scrum, and it remains one of the primary domains where Scrum is extensively utilized. The principles of Agile and Scrum are inherently well-suited to the challenges faced by software development teams. Below are key aspects of Scrum's application in software development:

### Agile Software Development

Scrum is a cornerstone of Agile software development methodologies. Agile emphasizes customer collaboration, continuous delivery of valuable software, and responsiveness to change. Scrum helps software development teams achieve these goals through its structured framework.

### Cross-Functional Teams

Scrum advocates for cross-functional teams comprising members with diverse skills, including developers, testers, designers, and product owners. This diversity enables teams to tackle complex software development tasks effectively.

### Sprint-Based Development

Software development in Scrum is organized into time-boxed iterations called sprints. Sprints typically last two to four weeks and result in potentially shippable increments of the product. This iterative approach allows teams to adapt to evolving requirements and deliver value at regular intervals.

### Backlog Management

The product backlog, a prioritized list of features and user stories, serves as the roadmap for software development. The product owner manages the backlog, ensuring that the team works on the most valuable items first.

### Daily Stand-ups

Daily stand-up meetings, or daily scrums, are a hallmark of Scrum in software development. Team members gather to discuss progress, challenges, and plans for the day, fostering communication and alignment.

## Continuous Integration and Testing

Scrum promotes continuous integration, where code changes are integrated into the main codebase multiple times a day. Automated testing ensures that software remains reliable and bug-free.

## Retrospectives

At the end of each sprint, teams conduct retrospectives to reflect on their processes and identify areas for improvement. This iterative feedback loop enhances team performance and efficiency.

## Scaling Scrum

Large software development projects often require scaling Scrum to accommodate multiple teams. Frameworks like the Scaled Agile Framework (SAFe) and Large Scale Scrum (LeSS) offer guidelines for scaling Scrum effectively.

## Tools and Technologies

Software development teams leverage various tools and technologies to support their Scrum practices. Project management software, version control systems, and communication platforms facilitate collaboration and tracking progress.

## Agile Engineering Practices

In addition to Scrum's framework, Agile software development often incorporates engineering practices like test-driven development (TDD), pair programming, and continuous deployment. These practices promote code quality and responsiveness to change.

## Case Studies

Throughout this section, we will explore case studies and real-world examples of how Scrum has been applied in software development. These examples showcase the versatility of Scrum and its ability to drive success in a rapidly evolving industry.

In summary, Scrum has had a profound impact on the field of software development, enabling teams to deliver high-quality software efficiently while adapting to changing requirements. This section will delve deeper into the nuances and practical applications of Scrum in software development through case studies and insights from experienced practitioners.

While Scrum originated in the realm of software development, its principles and practices have found applications far beyond coding. One such domain is marketing, where Scrum's agile approach to project management and collaboration has proven highly effective.

### Agile Marketing

Agile marketing, inspired by the Agile Manifesto, is a mindset and approach that values customer collaboration, adaptability, and data-driven decision-making. Scrum serves as a practical framework for implementing Agile principles in marketing.

### Scrum in Marketing Teams

Marketing teams deal with various tasks, from content creation and campaign planning to social media management and data analysis. Scrum helps marketing teams prioritize and manage their workload effectively.

### Sprint-Based Marketing

Just as in software development, marketing teams can benefit from working in time-boxed iterations or sprints. These sprints, often two to four weeks long, enable marketers to focus on high-priority tasks and adapt to changing market conditions.

### Backlog Management

In marketing, the product backlog is replaced by a marketing backlog, a prioritized list of tasks, campaigns, and initiatives. The marketing manager or product owner maintains the backlog, ensuring alignment with strategic goals.

### Daily Stand-ups

Daily stand-up meetings are a key practice in Scrum for marketing teams. Team members gather to discuss progress, share insights, and address any blockers. This brief daily interaction fosters collaboration and keeps the team aligned.

### Data-Driven Marketing

Scrum encourages data-driven decision-making. Marketers use analytics tools and metrics to assess the effectiveness of campaigns, gather customer feedback, and adjust their strategies accordingly.

### Retrospectives in Marketing

At the end of each sprint, marketing teams conduct retrospectives to reflect on their performance. They analyze what worked, what didn't, and how to improve in the next sprint. This continuous feedback loop drives marketing excellence.

In large marketing departments or agencies, scaling Scrum may be necessary. Teams can employ frameworks like SAFe for Marketing or adapt Scrum's principles to suit their specific needs.

## Marketing Technology Stack

Marketing teams leverage a variety of tools and technologies, including customer relationship management (CRM) systems, email marketing platforms, social media management tools, and data analytics software. These tools aid in campaign execution, measurement, and optimization.

## Agile Content Creation

Content marketing is a core aspect of modern marketing. Agile content creation, which aligns with Scrum's principles, involves creating and publishing content in short, iterative cycles to stay relevant and responsive to audience needs.

## Case Studies

Throughout this section, we will explore case studies and examples of how Scrum has transformed marketing efforts. These real-world stories demonstrate how Agile marketing practices have led to improved customer engagement and ROI.

In summary, Scrum is not limited to software development but can be applied effectively in marketing. It enables marketing teams to work collaboratively, respond to market changes swiftly, and deliver campaigns that resonate with their audience. This section delves deeper into the practical implementation of Scrum in marketing and presents insights from successful Agile marketing initiatives.

---

## Section 9.3: Scrum in Manufacturing

Manufacturing, often associated with assembly lines and traditional project management, has seen a transformation in recent years with the adoption of Agile methodologies like Scrum. Applying Scrum principles to manufacturing processes can lead to improved efficiency, flexibility, and product quality.

## Agile Manufacturing

Agile manufacturing is an approach that emphasizes responsiveness to customer demands, rapid adaptation to changing market conditions, and collaboration among cross-functional teams. Scrum, with its focus on iterative development and continuous improvement, aligns well with the principles of Agile manufacturing.

## Scrum in Production Lines

In manufacturing, production lines are at the heart of the process. Scrum can be applied to optimize production line operations. Instead of fixed production plans, teams work in sprints to meet customer demands while maintaining high product quality.

## Sprint-Based Manufacturing

Sprints, typically one to four weeks long, are used in manufacturing to address specific production goals. Teams plan their work for the sprint, monitor progress, and make adjustments as needed to meet targets and respond to changes in demand.

## Product Backlog in Manufacturing

In Scrum for manufacturing, the product backlog contains a list of items that need to be produced or tasks that must be completed. These items are prioritized based on customer orders, market demand, and other factors.

## Daily Stand-ups in Manufacturing

Just as in software development, daily stand-up meetings are essential in manufacturing. Team members gather to discuss production status, identify bottlenecks, and ensure a smooth workflow. This practice enhances communication and problem-solving.

## Lean Principles

Scrum in manufacturing often incorporates Lean principles, which aim to eliminate waste and improve efficiency. Lean tools and techniques, such as value stream mapping and 5S methodology, complement Scrum practices to create a lean-agile manufacturing environment.

## Continuous Improvement

Manufacturing teams using Scrum regularly conduct retrospectives to assess their processes and identify areas for improvement. This iterative feedback loop fosters a culture of continuous improvement, leading to more efficient production.

## Scaling Scrum in Manufacturing

Large manufacturing facilities or organizations with multiple production lines may need to scale Scrum. They can do so by implementing frameworks like SAFe for Manufacturing or by customizing Scrum practices to suit their specific manufacturing needs.

## Automation and Technology

Manufacturing is increasingly incorporating automation and technology to streamline processes. Scrum teams in manufacturing can leverage these advancements to enhance productivity and quality control.

Quality control and inspection processes are integral to manufacturing. Scrum teams focus on maintaining high product quality through rigorous testing, inspections, and adherence to quality standards.

## Case Studies

Throughout this section, we will explore case studies and real-world examples of how Scrum has been successfully implemented in manufacturing settings. These case studies highlight the benefits of adopting Agile principles and Scrum practices in improving manufacturing outcomes.

In conclusion, Scrum is not limited to software development but can be adapted effectively to enhance manufacturing processes. By embracing Agile and Scrum principles, manufacturing teams can become more responsive to customer needs, reduce waste, and continuously improve their production capabilities. This section provides insights into the practical application of Scrum in manufacturing, along with inspiring success stories from the industry.

---

# Section 9.4: Scrum in Education

Education is undergoing a significant transformation with the adoption of Agile methodologies like Scrum. Educators and institutions are recognizing the value of Agile principles in enhancing learning experiences and preparing students for the rapidly changing world. In this section, we'll explore how Scrum is being applied in educational settings.

## Agile Learning

Agile learning is an approach that emphasizes adaptability, collaboration, and iterative improvement in education. It borrows from Agile and Scrum concepts to create a more dynamic and student-centric learning environment.

## Scrum in the Classroom

Scrum can be introduced in the classroom to promote active learning and student engagement. Teachers can act as Scrum Masters, and students as the Scrum Team. The curriculum becomes the product backlog, and sprints are used to achieve learning objectives.

## Student Empowerment

Scrum in education empowers students by giving them a voice in their learning process. They participate in sprint planning, set goals, and self-organize to complete tasks. This autonomy fosters a sense of responsibility and ownership over their education.

### Collaboration and Communication

Scrum encourages collaboration among students. Daily stand-up meetings provide a platform for students to share progress, discuss challenges, and support each other. This communication helps build a sense of community within the classroom.

### Sprint-Based Learning

Similar to software development, education can benefit from a sprint-based approach. Teachers and students work together in short cycles (sprints) to achieve specific learning outcomes. At the end of each sprint, there's a review to reflect on what was learned and what can be improved.

### Adaptation to Student Needs

Scrum allows educators to adapt quickly to the changing needs and abilities of students. If a particular topic requires more attention, it can be prioritized for the next sprint. This flexibility ensures that learning remains relevant and engaging.

### Scrum in Higher Education

Scrum is not limited to primary and secondary education; it's also making its way into higher education. Universities and colleges are adopting Agile and Scrum practices to improve curriculum design, project-based learning, and research initiatives.

### Continuous Improvement

Retrospectives are a key component of Scrum in education. Teachers and students come together to reflect on the learning process, identify areas for improvement, and make adjustments for the next sprint. This iterative feedback loop leads to continuous improvement in teaching and learning.

### Challenges in Implementing Scrum in Education

While Scrum offers many benefits in education, there are challenges to overcome. These include resistance to change, the need for proper training, and aligning Scrum practices with educational standards and regulations.

### Case Studies

Throughout this section, we will explore case studies and real-world examples of how Scrum has been successfully implemented in educational settings. These case studies highlight the positive impact of Agile learning on student engagement, performance, and overall educational outcomes.

In summary, Scrum is transforming the education landscape by promoting Agile learning, student empowerment, and collaboration. Educators who embrace Scrum principles are better equipped to adapt to the evolving needs of students and create engaging learning experiences. This section provides insights into the practical application of Scrum in education, along with inspiring success stories from educational institutions around the world.

---

## Section 9.5: Scrum in Non-Profit Organizations

The principles of Scrum are not limited to the corporate world or for-profit businesses. Non-profit organizations have also found value in adopting Agile and Scrum practices to improve their operations and achieve their missions more effectively. In this section, we will explore how Scrum is being applied in the non-profit sector.

### Agile for Social Impact

Non-profit organizations often deal with complex social issues, and their work is driven by a desire to create positive change in society. Agile methodologies, including Scrum, provide a framework for these organizations to respond quickly to evolving needs, collaborate with stakeholders, and measure the impact of their initiatives.

### Scrum in Project Management

Non-profits frequently manage projects, whether they involve community outreach, fundraising campaigns, or humanitarian efforts. Scrum can be adapted to the project management needs of non-profit organizations, enabling them to deliver results efficiently and transparently.

### Collaborative Fundraising

Fundraising is a critical activity for non-profits, and Scrum principles can be applied to fundraising campaigns. Scrum teams, consisting of fundraisers, marketers, and other stakeholders, can work collaboratively to plan and execute campaigns, set fundraising goals, and adapt their strategies based on donor feedback and campaign performance.

### Volunteer Engagement

Many non-profit organizations rely on volunteers to support their missions. Scrum can help in managing volunteer teams by providing a structured approach to task allocation, progress tracking, and volunteer training. This results in a more engaged and effective volunteer workforce.

### Transparency and Accountability

Scrum promotes transparency through practices like daily stand-up meetings and sprint reviews. For non-profits, transparency is crucial in demonstrating accountability to donors, beneficiaries, and the broader community. By showcasing their progress and results, non-profit organizations can build trust and support.

### Empowering Stakeholders

Scrum empowers stakeholders to have a say in the direction of projects and initiatives. In non-profits, this empowerment extends to beneficiaries, community members, and volunteers. By involving these stakeholders in the decision-making process, non-profit organizations can ensure their efforts align with the actual needs of those they serve.

### Impact Measurement

Non-profits are increasingly focused on measuring their impact and outcomes. Scrum's iterative approach allows organizations to collect and analyze data regularly, enabling them to make data-driven decisions and refine their strategies to maximize their positive impact on society.

### Challenges and Considerations

While Scrum offers valuable benefits to non-profit organizations, there are challenges to consider. These include limited resources, the need for training and coaching, and adapting Scrum practices to the unique context of non-profit work. Overcoming these challenges requires commitment and a clear understanding of how Agile and Scrum can be applied effectively.

### Real-World Examples

Throughout this section, we will highlight real-world examples of non-profit organizations that have successfully implemented Scrum and Agile practices. These case studies will illustrate the diverse ways in which Scrum can be applied to address social and humanitarian challenges, from disaster relief efforts to community development projects.

In conclusion, Scrum is not exclusive to the business world; it has found a valuable place in non-profit organizations seeking to make a positive impact on society. By embracing Agile principles and Scrum practices, non-profits can enhance their ability to collaborate, adapt, and achieve meaningful outcomes for the communities and causes they serve. This section provides insights into the practical application of Scrum in the non-profit sector and showcases inspiring stories of social impact achieved through Agile approaches.

---

# Chapter 10: The Human Side of Scrum

## Section 10.1: Emotional Intelligence in Scrum Leadership

Emotional intelligence (EI) plays a significant role in the success of Scrum Masters and Agile leaders. While technical skills are essential, it's the ability to understand, manage, and leverage emotions that truly sets exceptional Scrum Masters apart. In this section, we delve into the importance of emotional intelligence in the context of Scrum leadership.

### Understanding Emotional Intelligence

Emotional intelligence encompasses several components, including self-awareness, self-regulation, empathy, and social skills. Scrum Masters who excel in these areas are better equipped to navigate the complex dynamics of Agile teams and foster a positive, productive environment.

### Self-Awareness for Scrum Masters

Self-awareness is the foundation of emotional intelligence. Scrum Masters should have a deep understanding of their own emotions, strengths, and weaknesses. This self-awareness allows them to stay composed under pressure, make informed decisions, and set a positive example for their teams.

### Self-Regulation and Resilience

In the fast-paced world of Scrum, challenges and setbacks are inevitable. Scrum Masters with high emotional intelligence can regulate their emotions effectively. They bounce back from setbacks, remain adaptable in changing circumstances, and maintain a constructive attitude, even when faced with adversity.

### Empathy and Team Relationships

Empathy is a critical skill for Scrum Masters. It involves understanding the emotions and perspectives of team members and stakeholders. By demonstrating empathy, Scrum Masters build trust, foster collaboration, and create a safe space for open communication within the team.

### Social Skills and Influence

Effective Scrum Masters possess strong social skills. They excel in communication, conflict resolution, and negotiation. They can influence and inspire their teams, removing impediments and facilitating progress. Their ability to build rapport and trust is invaluable in promoting team cohesion and achieving project goals.

## Motivating Agile Teams

Motivating Agile teams requires emotional intelligence. Scrum Masters should recognize and reward team members' contributions, provide constructive feedback, and create an environment where individuals feel valued and motivated to excel.

## Dealing with Conflict and Difficult Conversations

Conflict is a natural part of any team. Scrum Masters with high emotional intelligence can address conflicts constructively. They facilitate difficult conversations, mediate disputes, and help the team find mutually beneficial solutions.

## Emotional Intelligence Assessment

Assessing emotional intelligence can be a valuable tool for Scrum Masters. Various assessments and tools are available to measure and improve emotional intelligence, providing insights into areas that may need development.

## Training and Development

Emotional intelligence can be cultivated and developed over time. Scrum Masters can benefit from training, workshops, and coaching to enhance their emotional intelligence skills. These programs help them become more effective leaders and better support their Agile teams.

## Real-World Examples

Throughout this section, we will explore real-world examples of Scrum Masters and Agile leaders who have leveraged emotional intelligence to overcome challenges, lead high-performing teams, and achieve outstanding results in Agile projects. These stories illustrate the practical application of emotional intelligence in Scrum leadership.

In conclusion, emotional intelligence is a crucial asset for Scrum Masters and Agile leaders. It empowers them to build strong relationships, navigate challenges gracefully, and inspire their teams to reach new heights. This section provides insights into the significance of emotional intelligence in Scrum leadership and offers practical guidance for Scrum Masters looking to develop and leverage this essential skill set.

---

## Section 10.2: Building Trust and Transparency

Trust and transparency are fundamental elements of effective Scrum leadership. In this section, we delve into the importance of these aspects and how Scrum Masters can foster them within their Agile teams.

Trust is the cornerstone of any successful team. It's the belief that team members can rely on each other to accomplish their goals. Scrum Masters play a pivotal role in establishing and maintaining trust within their teams.

## Leading by Example

Scrum Masters must lead by example to build trust. They should demonstrate integrity, honesty, and accountability in their actions and decisions. When team members see their Scrum Master embodying these values, it sets a positive standard for the entire team.

## Open and Honest Communication

Transparent communication is essential in Scrum. Scrum Masters should encourage open and honest discussions within the team. They should create an environment where team members feel comfortable sharing their ideas, concerns, and challenges without fear of judgment.

## Managing Expectations

Clear expectations are key to building trust. Scrum Masters should ensure that team members understand their roles, responsibilities, and the goals of each sprint or project. When everyone is on the same page, trust is naturally reinforced.

## Conflict Resolution

Conflict is inevitable in any team. Scrum Masters should address conflicts promptly and constructively. By mediating disputes and helping the team find resolutions, they prevent conflicts from eroding trust.

## Trust in Decision-Making

Scrum Masters often facilitate decision-making processes within the team. It's crucial that team members trust their Scrum Master's judgment. This trust is built by consistently making well-informed, fair decisions that prioritize the team's success.

## Empowering the Team

Trust is also built by empowering the team to make decisions autonomously. Scrum Masters should trust their team members' expertise and allow them the freedom to take ownership of their work. This empowerment fosters a sense of responsibility and accountability among team members.

## Transparency in Work and Progress

Transparency goes hand-in-hand with trust. Scrum Masters should ensure that work progress, impediments, and challenges are visible to the team. Transparency allows team members to assess the situation accurately and collaborate effectively.

Agile metrics, such as burndown charts and velocity tracking, provide transparency into project progress. Scrum Masters should use these metrics to keep the team informed about their performance and to identify areas for improvement.

### Handling Mistakes and Failures

Trust is not just about successes; it's also about how teams handle mistakes and failures. Scrum Masters should create an environment where errors are seen as opportunities for learning and growth, rather than sources of blame.

### Trust and Collaboration

A high level of trust enables effective collaboration within the team. Team members are more likely to share knowledge, offer assistance, and collaborate on problem-solving when they trust their colleagues and Scrum Master.

### Case Studies

This section will feature case studies and real-world examples of Scrum Masters who have successfully built trust and transparency within their Agile teams. These stories will illustrate how trust and transparency contributed to the team's success and provide practical insights for Scrum Masters looking to enhance these aspects of their leadership.

In summary, trust and transparency are vital components of Scrum leadership. Scrum Masters who prioritize these elements create an environment where teams can thrive, collaborate effectively, and deliver outstanding results. This section explores the strategies and practices that Scrum Masters can employ to build trust and promote transparency within their Agile teams.

---

## Section 10.3: The Psychology of Team Dynamics

Understanding the psychology of team dynamics is essential for Scrum Masters. Successful Scrum Masters are not just facilitators of processes; they are also experts in navigating the complex world of human behavior and group interactions within Agile teams.

### Forming, Storming, Norming, Performing

Teams go through stages of development, as described by Bruce W. Tuckman in his Forming-Storming-Norming-Performing model. Scrum Masters should be aware of these stages and know how to support their teams accordingly:

- **Forming:** In this initial stage, team members are getting to know each other. They may be polite and cautious, as they're uncertain about their roles and the project's goals. Scrum Masters can help by facilitating introductions and setting clear expectations.

- **Storming:** As the team starts working together, conflicts and differences of opinion can arise. This is a crucial phase where team dynamics are tested. Scrum Masters should encourage healthy debates and help resolve conflicts constructively.

- **Norming:** During this stage, the team begins to establish norms and processes. Roles become clearer, and trust starts to develop. Scrum Masters can reinforce positive behaviors and support the team in solidifying their norms.

- **Performing:** In the performing stage, the team is highly productive, and members collaborate seamlessly. Scrum Masters should maintain a supportive role, ensuring that the team has what it needs to excel.

## Psychological Safety

Psychological safety is a critical aspect of team dynamics. It refers to an environment where team members feel safe to take risks, voice their opinions, and be themselves without fear of negative consequences. Scrum Masters should actively cultivate psychological safety within their teams:

- **Encouraging Participation:** Scrum Masters should create an atmosphere where all team members are encouraged to speak up, share ideas, and contribute without the fear of criticism.

- **Respecting Diversity:** Teams often consist of individuals with diverse backgrounds, perspectives, and skills. Scrum Masters should celebrate this diversity and ensure that all voices are heard and valued.

- **Leading by Example:** Scrum Masters should model the behaviors they want to see in their teams. When they demonstrate vulnerability and admit their mistakes, it encourages others to do the same.

## Motivation and Engagement

Understanding what motivates team members is crucial for a Scrum Master. Motivated team members are more engaged, productive, and committed to achieving team goals. Some key principles related to motivation include:

- **Autonomy:** Team members value having some control over their work. Scrum Masters should allow for autonomy in decision-making whenever possible.

- **Mastery:** People are motivated by the opportunity to develop their skills and become experts in their field. Scrum Masters should support team members in their quest for mastery.

- **Purpose:** Knowing the purpose and impact of their work motivates individuals. Scrum Masters should ensure that team members understand how their contributions align with the overall project and company goals.

Conflict is a natural part of team dynamics. Scrum Masters should have conflict resolution skills to address issues promptly and effectively:

- **Active Listening:** Scrum Masters should listen actively to understand the root causes of conflicts and concerns.

- **Mediation:** When conflicts escalate, Scrum Masters may need to mediate discussions and help parties find common ground.

- **Negotiation:** Scrum Masters should be skilled negotiators, helping team members reach compromises and solutions that benefit everyone.

- **Feedback:** Constructive feedback is essential for conflict resolution. Scrum Masters should provide feedback that focuses on behaviors and outcomes, not personalities.

Team Building Activities

Team building activities can be valuable tools for improving team dynamics. Scrum Masters can organize activities that promote collaboration, communication, and trust among team members. These activities can range from icebreakers and team retrospectives to off-site events and workshops.

In conclusion, the psychology of team dynamics is a multifaceted aspect of Scrum Masters' roles. Understanding team development stages, fostering psychological safety, motivating team members, and effectively resolving conflicts are all essential components of successful Scrum leadership. Scrum Masters who grasp the intricacies of team psychology can guide their teams to higher levels of performance and collaboration.

---

## Section 10.4: Motivating and Inspiring Agile Teams

Motivating and inspiring Agile teams is a fundamental aspect of a Scrum Master's role. Agile methodologies thrive on self-organizing, motivated teams that take ownership of their work and deliver value consistently. In this section, we will explore various strategies and techniques that Scrum Masters can employ to keep their Agile teams motivated and inspired.

### 1. Setting Clear Goals and Objectives:

Providing the team with clear, well-defined goals and objectives helps create a sense of purpose and direction. When team members understand the broader vision and how their work contributes to it, they are more motivated to excel.

Agile teams perform best when they have a degree of autonomy in decision-making. Scrum Masters should empower team members to make choices about how they work, collaborate, and solve problems. Autonomy increases a sense of ownership and responsibility.

### 3. Supporting Mastery:

Motivated individuals are driven by the desire to improve and master their skills. Scrum Masters should encourage continuous learning and provide opportunities for team members to enhance their expertise. This can be through training, mentoring, or knowledge-sharing sessions.

### 4. Celebrating Achievements:

Recognizing and celebrating the team's achievements, no matter how small, boosts morale and motivation. Acknowledging individual and collective successes reinforces a positive work environment.

### 5. Providing Constructive Feedback:

Feedback plays a crucial role in motivation. Scrum Masters should offer regular, constructive feedback that highlights strengths and areas for improvement. Effective feedback helps individuals understand their progress and make necessary adjustments.

### 6. Creating a Safe Environment:

A psychologically safe environment is one where team members feel comfortable taking risks, asking questions, and sharing their thoughts and concerns. Scrum Masters should actively work to establish and maintain this safety within the team.

### 7. Encouraging Collaboration:

Collaboration fosters a sense of belonging and camaraderie among team members. Scrum Masters should encourage open communication and collaboration, helping team members build strong working relationships.

### 8. Recognizing Individual Contributions:

While Agile teams work collaboratively, it's essential to recognize and appreciate individual contributions. Scrum Masters should ensure that each team member feels valued and that their unique skills are acknowledged.

### 9. Setting Realistic Expectations:

Unrealistic expectations can lead to frustration and demotivation. Scrum Masters should work with the team to set achievable goals and ensure that they have the resources and support needed to meet those expectations.

### 10. Continuous Improvement Culture:

Agile teams thrive in environments where continuous improvement is encouraged. Scrum Masters should facilitate retrospectives and other feedback mechanisms to identify areas for improvement and support the team in making necessary changes.

### 11. Lead by Example:

Scrum Masters should model the behaviors and attitudes they want to see in their teams. Being a role model of motivation, commitment, and professionalism can inspire team members to follow suit.

### 12. Understanding Individual Motivations:

Different team members may be motivated by different factors. Some may value recognition, while others prioritize personal growth. Scrum Masters should take the time to understand what motivates each team member individually and tailor their approach accordingly.

### 13. Maintaining Work-Life Balance:

Burnout can quickly lead to demotivation. Scrum Masters should help team members strike a healthy work-life balance by monitoring workloads, encouraging breaks, and addressing signs of burnout promptly.

### 14. Adapting to Changing Needs:

Agile teams and individuals evolve over time. Scrum Masters should be flexible and adapt their motivational strategies to accommodate changing needs and circumstances.

### 15. Seeking Continuous Feedback:

Scrum Masters should actively seek feedback from team members about their motivational strategies. This feedback loop ensures that the approaches used are effective and can be adjusted as needed.

In summary, motivating and inspiring Agile teams is an ongoing process that requires a deep understanding of individual and team dynamics. Scrum Masters who excel in this aspect of their role can create high-performing teams that consistently deliver value and embrace Agile principles.

---

## Section 10.5: Dealing with Burnout and Team Fatigue

Burnout and team fatigue are critical issues that Scrum Masters must address to maintain a healthy and productive Agile team. Prolonged periods of stress and overwork can lead to reduced morale, lower productivity, and high turnover rates. In this section, we'll explore strategies for recognizing, preventing, and addressing burnout and team fatigue within Agile teams.

## 1. Recognizing Burnout Symptoms:

The first step in dealing with burnout is recognizing its symptoms. These can include increased cynicism, decreased motivation, chronic fatigue, decreased quality of work, and emotional exhaustion. Scrum Masters should be vigilant for these signs in team members.

## 2. Encourage Open Communication:

Create an environment where team members feel comfortable discussing their concerns and stress levels openly. Regular one-on-one meetings can provide a platform for team members to express their feelings and seek support.

## 3. Balance Workload:

Ensure that workloads are evenly distributed among team members. Use Agile principles like capacity planning to avoid overburdening individuals. If necessary, adjust sprint goals or deadlines to maintain a sustainable pace.

## 4. Promote Work-Life Balance:

Encourage team members to maintain a healthy work-life balance. Emphasize the importance of taking breaks, using vacation time, and disconnecting from work outside of office hours.

## 5. Provide Training and Skill Development:

Sometimes, team members may feel burnout if they lack the necessary skills to perform their roles effectively. Offer training opportunities and resources to help team members build competence and confidence.

## 6. Flexibility and Adaptation:

Be flexible in accommodating individual needs and personal circumstances. Life events or external pressures can contribute to burnout, and showing understanding in such situations can make a significant difference.

## 7. Delegate Responsibilities:

Ensure that team members are not shouldering an excessive number of responsibilities. Delegate tasks and responsibilities appropriately, taking into account each team member's capacity and skills.

## 8. Celebrate Achievements:

Acknowledge and celebrate team achievements regularly. Recognizing successes, no matter how small, boosts morale and reminds team members of their collective accomplishments.

## 9. Encourage Self-Care:

Promote self-care practices such as exercise, mindfulness, and stress management techniques. Encourage team members to prioritize their well-being and provide resources or recommendations for self-care.

## 10. Team Building Activities:

Organize team-building activities and events to strengthen camaraderie and create a positive team culture. These activities can provide opportunities for team members to relax and bond.

## 11. Rotate Roles and Responsibilities:

Allow team members to rotate roles within the team if feasible. This can prevent monotony and burnout by giving individuals a fresh perspective and new challenges.

## 12. Address Conflicts Promptly:

Unresolved conflicts can contribute to team fatigue. Scrum Masters should address conflicts promptly and help team members find constructive resolutions.

## 13. Implement Time Management Techniques:

Teach time management techniques to help team members prioritize tasks, set realistic goals, and manage their work effectively. This can reduce the stress associated with tight deadlines.

## 14. Monitor Work Hours:

Keep an eye on team members' work hours, especially during sprints. Ensure that overtime is not becoming the norm and that team members have the opportunity to rest.

## 15. Seek Feedback and Adjust:

Continuously seek feedback from team members about their workload, stress levels, and the effectiveness of implemented strategies. Be prepared to adjust your approach based on their input.

## 16. Lead by Example:

Scrum Masters should set an example by managing their own workload and stress levels effectively. Demonstrating self-care practices and a healthy work-life balance can inspire the team to do the same.

## 17. Consult HR or Mental Health Professionals:

In cases of severe burnout or emotional distress, consider involving human resources or mental health professionals to provide support and resources to affected team members.

Addressing burnout and team fatigue is essential for maintaining a motivated and healthy Agile team. Scrum Masters play a vital role in creating an environment that promotes well-being, reduces stress, and fosters resilience, ultimately contributing to the team's success and long-term satisfaction.

# Chapter 11: Agile Metrics and Reporting

## Section 11.1: Key Metrics for Scrum Teams

Agile metrics play a crucial role in assessing the performance and health of Scrum teams. They provide valuable insights into the team's progress, efficiency, and overall effectiveness. By tracking and analyzing these metrics, Scrum Masters and stakeholders can make informed decisions, identify areas for improvement, and ensure that the project is on the right track. In this section, we will explore some of the key metrics commonly used in Scrum and Agile environments.

### 1. Velocity

Velocity is one of the fundamental metrics in Scrum. It measures the amount of work a team can complete in a single sprint. Velocity is usually expressed in story points, which are a unit of estimation for user stories or tasks. By tracking velocity over multiple sprints, teams can establish a predictable cadence for their work and better plan future sprints.

To calculate velocity, sum up the story points of all completed user stories or tasks during a sprint. It's essential to maintain consistency in story point estimation across sprints for accurate velocity measurements.

```
Velocity = Sum of Story Points Completed in a Sprint
```

### 2. Burndown Chart

A burndown chart is a visual representation of the remaining work in a sprint. It helps the team track progress and understand if they are on track to complete all planned work by the end of the sprint. Burndown charts are particularly useful for identifying potential scope creep or delays.

The x-axis of the chart represents time (sprint days), while the y-axis represents the remaining work (usually in story points). A typical burndown chart starts at the total estimated effort for the sprint and should ideally trend towards zero as work gets completed.

### 3. Burnup Chart

Similar to the burndown chart, a burnup chart tracks work progress but also includes the total scope of the sprint. It helps teams visualize how the scope may change during the sprint due to new additions or scope reductions. By comparing the burnup and burndown charts, teams can gain a holistic view of the sprint's progress.

The x-axis of the burnup chart represents time (sprint days), and the y-axis represents both completed work and the total scope of the sprint. This chart helps teams make informed decisions about scope changes during the sprint.

## 4. Sprint Goal Success Rate

The sprint goal success rate measures how often a team successfully achieves the goals set for each sprint. Sprint goals are essential for providing a clear focus and purpose for the team during a sprint. A high success rate indicates that the team consistently meets its objectives.

To calculate the sprint goal success rate, divide the number of sprints in which all goals were achieved by the total number of sprints.

```
Sprint Goal Success Rate = (Number of Sprints with All Goals Achieved) / (Total Number of Sprints)
```

## 5. Lead Time and Cycle Time

Lead time and cycle time are essential metrics for understanding the efficiency of a Scrum team's workflow. Lead time measures the total time it takes from the moment a task is created until it is completed. Cycle time, on the other hand, measures the time it takes to complete a task once active work begins on it.

Reducing lead time and cycle time can lead to faster delivery of value to stakeholders. These metrics are often used in Kanban and Lean practices but can also be valuable in Scrum.

## 6. Sprint Review Feedback

Sprint reviews are an integral part of Scrum, where the team demonstrates the completed work to stakeholders and gathers feedback. The quality and quantity of feedback received during sprint reviews can be a valuable metric. It reflects the level of engagement and collaboration between the team and stakeholders.

Teams can track feedback received, categorize it, and use it to drive improvements in subsequent sprints. High-quality feedback can lead to more refined product increments.

## 7. Escaped Defects

Escaped defects are issues or bugs that were not detected within the sprint but are discovered later, often by end-users. Tracking escaped defects is essential for assessing the quality of the product increment and the effectiveness of the team's testing and quality assurance practices.

Teams should aim to minimize the number of escaped defects by improving their testing processes and ensuring that thorough testing is conducted during the sprint.

In conclusion, these metrics provide valuable insights into the performance and health of Scrum teams. It's essential to use a combination of these metrics to gain a comprehensive understanding of the team's progress and to continuously improve the Scrum process. However, teams should be cautious not to use metrics in a way that encourages undesirable behavior or puts undue pressure on team members. Agile metrics should always serve the goal of delivering value to customers and stakeholders.

Burndown charts are a powerful tool in Agile and Scrum methodologies for tracking the progress of work during a sprint. They provide a visual representation of how much work remains to be completed in a sprint, helping Scrum teams stay on top of their commitments and make informed decisions. In this section, we will delve into the effective use of burndown charts and the insights they can offer.

## Understanding Burndown Charts

Burndown charts typically consist of two axes: the horizontal axis represents time (usually sprint days), and the vertical axis represents the amount of work remaining (often in story points). At the start of a sprint, the burndown chart begins at the total estimated effort for the sprint.

As the sprint progresses, the chart should ideally trend downwards towards zero, indicating that work is getting completed. The rate at which the chart descends can provide valuable insights into the team's pace and whether they are likely to complete all planned work by the end of the sprint.

## Benefits of Burndown Charts

1. **Visibility**: Burndown charts provide transparency into the team's progress. It's easy to see if the team is ahead, behind, or on track to meet their sprint commitments.

2. **Early Warning**: A sudden increase in the burndown rate or a plateau can serve as an early warning sign that something may be amiss in the sprint. This can prompt the team to take corrective action promptly.

3. **Scope Changes**: If additional work is added during the sprint (scope change), the burndown chart will reflect it. This allows the team to gauge the impact of scope changes on their ability to meet the sprint goal.

4. **Motivation**: Burndown charts can motivate the team to stay focused and strive to complete the work within the sprint. It provides a sense of accomplishment as the chart progresses downwards.

## Interpreting Burndown Charts

Interpreting burndown charts requires an understanding of different patterns and what they signify:

- **Ideal Burndown**: In an ideal world, the chart would have a linear decline towards zero. This indicates that work is being completed at a consistent rate, and the team is on track to finish everything planned.

- **Flat or Uptick**: If the burndown chart flattens or starts to move upwards, it suggests that the team is falling behind schedule. This may necessitate discussions about what's causing the delay and how to address it.

- **Steeper Than Ideal**: A burndown chart that descends faster than expected might indicate that the team initially overestimated the amount of work. It's essential to maintain a sustainable pace rather than rush through tasks.

- **Scope Change**: If there's a sudden spike or drop in the burndown chart, it's likely due to scope changes. Teams should track these changes separately to understand their impact.

- **Incomplete Work**: If the burndown chart does not reach zero by the end of the sprint, there is incomplete work. Teams should discuss this during the sprint review and assess why it occurred.

## Using Burndown Charts for Improvement

Burndown charts are not just for tracking progress; they can be instrumental in driving continuous improvement:

- **Retrospectives**: Teams can use burndown charts as a reference point during sprint retrospectives to discuss what went well and what didn't. It can help identify areas for improvement.

- **Process Adjustments**: If trends in burndown charts consistently show issues, such as a plateau at the end of every sprint, it may be time to adjust the team's processes or address bottlenecks.

- **Predictability**: Over time, a Scrum team can use historical burndown data to become more predictable in their commitments and better estimate how much work they can realistically complete in a sprint.

In conclusion, burndown charts are a valuable tool for Agile and Scrum teams to monitor their progress, identify potential issues, and drive continuous improvement. When used effectively, they promote transparency and accountability within the team and help deliver value to stakeholders consistently. However, it's crucial to remember that burndown charts are just one aspect of Agile metrics, and teams should use a combination of metrics for a holistic view of their performance.

---

## Section 11.3: Velocity Tracking and Capacity Planning

Velocity tracking and capacity planning are essential aspects of Agile and Scrum that enable teams to better manage their work, set realistic expectations, and continuously improve their performance. In this section, we will explore the concepts of velocity and capacity, how they are calculated, and their significance in Agile project management.

## Understanding Velocity

Velocity is a metric used in Scrum to measure the amount of work a team can complete in a single sprint. It is expressed in story points, ideal days, or another unit of effort, depending on the team's preference. Velocity provides a basis for predictability, helping teams understand how much work they can take on in future sprints.

Velocity is calculated by summing up the story points or effort units of all the user stories and tasks completed in a sprint. For instance, if a team completes user stories with a total of 30 story points in a two-week sprint, their velocity for that sprint is 30 story points. Over time, teams establish a consistent velocity that reflects their sustainable pace.

## Benefits of Tracking Velocity

1. **Predictability**: Velocity allows teams to forecast how much work they can complete in upcoming sprints. This helps stakeholders set realistic expectations about project timelines and deliverables.

2. **Capacity Planning**: By knowing their velocity, teams can commit to a sustainable amount of work in each sprint, preventing overloading and ensuring quality.

3. **Continuous Improvement**: Monitoring velocity over time provides insights into a team's performance trends. Teams can use this data to identify areas for improvement and make adjustments accordingly.

4. **Early Issue Detection**: Significant drops or variations in velocity can signal issues within the team, such as bottlenecks, scope creep, or resource constraints.

## Calculating Velocity

Velocity is calculated by adding up the story points or effort units of the completed work in a sprint. Here's a basic formula for calculating velocity:

$$\text{Velocity} = \sum \text{Story Points (or Effort Units) of Completed User Stories and Tasks} = \text{Velocity} = \sum \text{Story Points (or Effort Units) of Completed User Stories and Tasks}$$

It's important to note that only work items that are considered "done" at the end of the sprint should be included in the velocity calculation. Partially completed work or items that don't meet the team's definition of done should not be counted.

## Using Velocity for Capacity Planning

Capacity planning involves determining how much work a team can take on in an upcoming sprint based on their historical velocity. Here are the steps for capacity planning:

1. **Calculate Average Velocity**: Calculate the team's average velocity over the last several sprints. This provides a baseline for capacity planning.

2. **Consider Factors**: Take into account any factors that might affect capacity, such as holidays, team member availability, or external dependencies.

3. **Commit to Work**: Based on the calculated average velocity and considering any influencing factors, the team commits to a set of user stories and tasks for the next sprint.

4. **Monitor Progress**: During the sprint, the team monitors their progress using a burndown chart or other visual tools. If it becomes evident that they won't meet their commitment, adjustments can be made.

5. **Reflect and Adapt**: After the sprint, the team reflects on their performance and adjusts their capacity planning if necessary.

## Challenges with Velocity

While velocity is a valuable metric, it's essential to be aware of potential challenges:

- **Variance**: Velocity can vary from sprint to sprint, making it challenging to predict exact timelines.

- **External Factors**: External factors, such as changing project requirements, can impact velocity.

- **Team Changes**: Team changes, like adding or removing members, can also affect velocity.

In conclusion, velocity tracking and capacity planning are fundamental tools for Agile and Scrum teams to manage their work effectively. By understanding their velocity and using it for capacity planning, teams can deliver value consistently and improve their predictability over time. However, it's crucial to approach velocity as a guideline rather than a strict rule and to adapt as needed based on the team's unique circumstances.

---

## Section 11.4: Reporting to Stakeholders

Reporting to stakeholders is a critical aspect of Agile and Scrum project management. It ensures transparency, alignment of expectations, and provides valuable insights into project progress. In this section, we'll explore the significance of reporting, the types of reports commonly used, and best practices for effective communication with stakeholders.

## The Importance of Reporting

Effective reporting serves several purposes:

1.  **Transparency**: Reporting allows stakeholders to have visibility into the project's status, progress, and any potential issues. It builds trust and fosters an environment of openness.

2.  **Alignment**: It helps align stakeholders' expectations with the project's reality. When stakeholders have accurate information, they can make informed decisions and adjustments as needed.

3.  **Decision-Making**: Reports provide data-driven insights that aid in decision-making. They help prioritize work, allocate resources, and identify areas for improvement.

4.  **Risk Management**: Reporting can highlight risks and issues early on, allowing teams to take proactive measures to mitigate them.

## Common Types of Reports

1.  **Sprint Report**: This report summarizes the outcomes of a sprint, including completed user stories, velocity, and any unresolved issues. It is typically presented at the end of each sprint during the sprint review.

2.  **Burndown Chart**: Burndown charts visually represent the remaining work in a sprint over time. They help track progress and whether the team is on target to complete the planned work.

3.  **Release Report**: A release report provides an overview of the progress and status of a release or product increment. It may include features delivered, outstanding items, and release dates.

4.  **Backlog Report**: This report outlines the status of the product backlog, including the prioritization of user stories and any changes in backlog items.

5.  **Velocity Report**: Velocity reports show the team's historical velocity over multiple sprints. It helps stakeholders understand the team's capacity and predictability.

6.  **Risk Register**: A risk register lists identified risks, their likelihood, impact, and mitigation plans. It is essential for proactive risk management.

7.  **Stakeholder Updates**: Regular updates or newsletters to stakeholders can provide high-level information about the project's status, accomplishments, and upcoming milestones.

## Best Practices for Effective Reporting

1.  **Define Your Audience**: Tailor your reports to the specific needs and interests of your audience. Consider what information is most relevant to them.

2.  **Frequency**: Determine how often reports should be delivered. While sprint reports are typically at the end of each sprint, other reports may have different cadences.

3.  **Visualize Data**: Use charts, graphs, and visual aids to make data more accessible and understandable. Visual representations can convey information more effectively than raw numbers.

4.  **Narrative Context**: Provide a narrative that explains the data. Help stakeholders understand the story behind the numbers and any implications for the project.

5.  **Highlight Key Insights**: Identify and emphasize critical insights or trends within the data. Focus on what matters most to stakeholders.

6.  **Actionable Information**: Reports should not just inform but also prompt action. Include recommendations or action items based on the data presented.

7.  **Feedback Loop**: Encourage feedback from stakeholders to improve the reporting process continually. Ensure that the reports meet their needs and expectations.

8.  **Adaptability**: Be flexible in your reporting approach. As the project evolves, the types of reports and their content may need to change.

In summary, effective reporting to stakeholders is essential for successful Agile and Scrum projects. It promotes transparency, alignment, and informed decision-making. By tailoring reports to the audience, visualizing data, and providing context, project teams can ensure that stakeholders are well-informed and engaged throughout the project lifecycle.

---

## Section 11.5: Balancing Transparency and Privacy

Balancing transparency and privacy is a delicate challenge in Agile and Scrum projects. On one hand, Agile principles emphasize openness and sharing of information. On the other hand, there are legitimate concerns about privacy, data security, and confidentiality. In this section, we'll explore strategies for finding the right balance between transparency and privacy.

### The Dilemma of Transparency

Transparency is a core value in Agile, and it's essential for fostering trust and collaboration within a team and with stakeholders. However, there are instances where an excessive level of transparency can have negative consequences:

1.  **Confidential Information**: Some information, such as sensitive customer data, proprietary technology, or legal matters, must remain confidential for ethical, legal, or competitive reasons.

2.  **Security Risks**: Sharing too much information about a project's infrastructure or security measures can expose vulnerabilities that could be exploited by malicious actors.

3.  **Overload**: Providing too much data can overwhelm stakeholders and make it challenging to discern what's truly important.



1.  **Identify Sensitive Information**: Start by identifying what information should be treated as confidential. This includes customer data, intellectual property, security protocols, and legal matters. Create clear guidelines for handling and sharing this information only on a need-to-know basis.

2.  **Access Control**: Implement access control mechanisms to restrict who can access sensitive information. Use role-based access control (RBAC) or other access management systems to ensure that only authorized individuals can view or modify sensitive data.

3.  **Data Masking and Anonymization**: When sharing data for reporting or analysis, consider data masking or anonymization techniques. These methods replace sensitive information with placeholders or anonymized versions to protect privacy while still providing useful insights.

4.  **Aggregated Reporting**: Instead of sharing granular data, consider providing aggregated reports that summarize information without revealing specific details. For example, use summary statistics rather than individual records.

5.  **Limited Access to Historical Data**: Consider limiting access to historical project data. While it's important to learn from past experiences, not all team members or stakeholders need access to extensive historical records.

6.  **Communication Protocols**: Establish clear communication protocols for handling sensitive information. Define who can communicate certain types of information, how it should be communicated, and when it should be shared.

7.  **Education and Training**: Ensure that team members and stakeholders are educated about the importance of privacy and confidentiality. Provide training on data security best practices and the consequences of mishandling sensitive information.

8.  **Regular Audits**: Conduct regular audits of access and data sharing practices to identify any breaches or unauthorized disclosures. Address any issues promptly and reinforce privacy guidelines.

9.  **Legal and Regulatory Compliance**: Stay informed about relevant legal and regulatory requirements regarding data privacy and security. Ensure that your practices align with these standards.

10. **Ethical Considerations**: Consider the ethical implications of data sharing. Ask whether sharing specific information is in the best interest of all parties involved and whether it aligns with your organization's ethical values.

In conclusion, finding the right balance between transparency and privacy is essential for Agile and Scrum projects. While transparency promotes collaboration and trust, privacy safeguards sensitive information and mitigates risks. By implementing the strategies mentioned above, teams can navigate this delicate balance effectively and ensure that both transparency and privacy are maintained appropriately throughout the project lifecycle.

---

# Chapter 12: The Legal and Ethical Aspects of Scrum

## Section 12.1: Contract Management in Agile Projects

Agile and Scrum emphasize flexibility, adaptability, and collaboration, which can pose unique challenges when it comes to contract management. Traditional project management approaches often rely on detailed, fixed contracts, while Agile projects require a different approach that accommodates change and uncertainty. In this section, we'll explore how contract management fits into Agile projects and offer insights into best practices.

*Traditional Contracts vs. Agile Contracts*

In traditional project management, contracts tend to be based on fixed scopes, schedules, and costs. These contracts are less accommodating when changes are inevitable, as they often lead to disputes, delays, and additional costs when project requirements evolve.

Agile contracts, on the other hand, are designed to embrace change. They typically have the following characteristics:

1. **Iterative and Incremental**: Agile contracts acknowledge that requirements may evolve over time, and they are structured to accommodate changes through iterative development cycles.

2. **Value-Oriented**: Instead of focusing on detailed specifications, Agile contracts often prioritize delivering value to the customer. Payment milestones may be tied to the completion of specific features or increments of the product.

3. **Collaborative**: Agile contracts encourage collaboration between the client and the development team. Clients are typically involved in the development process, providing feedback and adjusting priorities.

*Types of Agile Contracts*

1. **Time and Materials (T&M)**: This type of contract is based on the actual time spent by the development team and the cost of materials (if any). T&M contracts provide flexibility but can be challenging to estimate in advance.

2. **Fixed-Price with Scope Flexibility**: These contracts have a fixed overall price but allow for changes in scope. Clients can reprioritize features or requirements within the fixed budget.

3. **Fixed-Price per Iteration**: Payments are tied to the completion of iterations or sprints. This aligns with Agile's incremental approach and ensures that the client receives potentially shippable increments at regular intervals.

*Key Considerations in Agile Contract Management*

1. **Clearly Defined Expectations**: Regardless of the contract type, it's essential to have clear expectations and objectives. Define the project's goals, scope, and success criteria to ensure alignment between the client and the development team.

2. **Flexible Pricing Models**: Consider using pricing models that align with Agile principles, such as T&M or fixed-price with scope flexibility. Ensure that payment schedules reflect the incremental delivery of value.

3. **Change Control Mechanisms**: Establish mechanisms for handling changes in requirements. Define how changes will be prioritized, estimated, and implemented, as well as how they will impact the project timeline and budget.

4. **Collaborative Governance**: Agile contracts require ongoing collaboration between the client and the development team. Set up regular checkpoints, reviews, and feedback loops to ensure that the project stays on track.

5. **Risk Sharing**: Consider how risks will be shared between the parties involved. Agile contracts often involve a degree of shared risk, with both the client and the development team sharing responsibility for project success.

6. **Legal and Regulatory Compliance**: Ensure that Agile contracts comply with legal and regulatory requirements in your industry or region. Consult legal experts to draft contracts that protect the interests of all parties involved.

In conclusion, contract management in Agile projects requires a shift in mindset from traditional fixed contracts to more flexible, collaborative, and value-oriented agreements. Agile contracts should support incremental delivery of value, accommodate changes, and promote ongoing collaboration between clients and development teams. By following best practices and aligning contracts with Agile principles, organizations can successfully manage projects in dynamic and evolving environments.

---

## Section 12.2: Intellectual Property Considerations

When engaging in Agile and Scrum projects, intellectual property (IP) considerations play a crucial role in protecting the rights and assets of both clients and development teams. Agile's iterative and collaborative nature can introduce unique challenges and opportunities regarding IP. In this section, we'll explore key aspects of IP management in Agile projects.

Determining who owns the intellectual property created during an Agile project is a critical initial step. Ownership rights may be influenced by several factors, including contractual agreements, employment relationships, and the specific nature of the work.

1.  **Client Ownership**: In many cases, clients will expect to own the IP generated as a result of the project. Clear contractual agreements should specify the transfer of IP rights upon project completion.

2.  **Joint Ownership**: In collaborative Agile projects, it's possible for both the client and the development team to have joint ownership of IP. Such agreements should outline the rights and responsibilities of each party regarding the shared IP.

3.  **Third-Party Components**: Agile projects often involve the use of third-party libraries, frameworks, or open-source software. Understanding and complying with the licensing terms of these components is essential to avoid legal issues.

*Protecting Client IP*

Clients may have existing IP or sensitive data that they need to protect during an Agile project. Consider the following measures:

1.  **Confidentiality Agreements**: Establish non-disclosure agreements (NDAs) to protect sensitive client information. Ensure that all team members, including third-party contractors, are aware of and bound by these agreements.

2.  **Data Security**: Implement robust data security measures to safeguard client data. Encryption, access controls, and secure storage should be part of the project's infrastructure.

3.  **Access Control**: Limit access to client-specific resources and data to only those team members who require it. Regularly review and audit access permissions.

*Open Source and Licensing Compliance*

Agile projects often leverage open-source software components to accelerate development. However, it's crucial to understand the licensing terms of these components to ensure compliance. Common open-source licenses include the MIT License, GNU General Public License (GPL), Apache License, and more.

1.  **License Identification**: Maintain an inventory of all open-source components used in the project, along with their associated licenses. This can be managed using tools like SPDX (Software Package Data Exchange) or manual tracking.

2.  **Compliance Checks**: Regularly review and assess compliance with open-source licenses. Ensure that the project's use of open-source software aligns with the respective license requirements.

3. **License Compatibility**: Be mindful of license compatibility issues when combining software components with different licenses. Some licenses may be incompatible and can create legal challenges.



Maintaining thorough documentation related to IP is essential for transparency and risk management:

1. **IP Logs**: Keep detailed records of IP-related decisions, agreements, and changes throughout the project's lifecycle. This includes minutes from meetings, emails, and signed contracts.

2. **Version Control**: Use version control systems to track changes to IP assets, such as code and documentation. This provides an audit trail of modifications.

3. **License Tracking**: Continuously update and monitor the project's license tracking and compliance records to mitigate risks associated with IP infringement.

In conclusion, managing intellectual property in Agile and Scrum projects requires careful consideration of ownership, licensing, and confidentiality. Clear contractual agreements, transparent documentation, and adherence to licensing requirements are crucial for protecting the interests of both clients and development teams. By addressing IP considerations proactively, organizations can navigate Agile projects while safeguarding valuable intellectual assets.

---

## Section 12.3: Ethical Dilemmas in Agile Environments

Ethics play a pivotal role in the world of Agile development. Agile methodologies prioritize values such as collaboration, transparency, and customer focus. However, as Agile teams navigate complex projects and evolving requirements, they may encounter ethical dilemmas that require careful consideration and resolution.

*Agile Principles and Ethical Values*

Agile principles inherently align with several ethical values:

1. **Customer Collaboration Over Contract Negotiation**: This Agile principle emphasizes building strong relationships with customers. Ethically, this means prioritizing customer needs and satisfaction, even when contract terms might suggest otherwise.

2. **Working Software Over Comprehensive Documentation**: Agile encourages delivering functional software quickly. Ethically, this aligns with the value of providing value to customers promptly, but it also raises questions about the quality and safety of the delivered software.

3. **Responding to Change Over Following a Plan**: Embracing change is fundamental in Agile. Ethically, this involves being adaptable and responsive to evolving customer needs, even if it disrupts the original plan.



1. **Quality vs. Speed**: Agile teams often face the dilemma of delivering software quickly while maintaining high quality. Balancing these priorities is an ethical consideration as compromising quality can harm users or lead to technical debt.

2. **Transparency vs. Confidentiality**: Agile advocates for transparency, but sometimes sensitive information must be kept confidential. Ethical decisions are required to determine what should be shared openly and what should remain confidential.

3. **Customer Satisfaction vs. Honesty**: Agile encourages collaboration with customers to meet their needs. However, if a customer's request contradicts ethical standards or best practices, Agile teams may face a dilemma between customer satisfaction and professional integrity.

4. **Team Morale vs. Accountability**: Agile teams rely on self-organizing and motivated individuals. Ethical concerns may arise when addressing accountability issues within the team, potentially affecting team morale.

5. **Client Expectations vs. Realistic Goals**: Managing client expectations is crucial, but sometimes clients have unrealistic expectations. Ethical dilemmas can arise when balancing the desire to please clients with the need for honesty about project limitations.



Addressing ethical dilemmas in Agile environments requires a systematic approach:

1. **Open Communication**: Encourage open and transparent communication within the team and with stakeholders. Discuss ethical concerns openly and seek input from all team members.

2. **Code of Ethics**: Develop and adhere to a clear code of ethics that outlines the values and principles that guide the team's decisions. This code can serve as a reference point when facing dilemmas.

3. **Ethics Training**: Provide ethics training to team members and stakeholders. Ensure that everyone understands the ethical values and principles underlying Agile methodologies.

4. **Ethics Committees**: Consider establishing ethics committees or review boards within the organization to address complex ethical dilemmas and provide guidance.

5. **Consultation**: Seek external consultation or legal advice when facing particularly challenging ethical dilemmas that have legal implications.

In conclusion, Agile environments present unique ethical challenges that require careful navigation. Ethical decision-making should be integrated into Agile practices to ensure that values such as customer satisfaction, transparency, and quality are upheld while also considering the broader ethical implications of project decisions. Agile teams that prioritize ethical considerations can build trust with stakeholders and foster a culture of integrity and responsibility.

---

## Section 12.4: Compliance and Regulatory Challenges

Agile development methodologies are widely adopted for their flexibility and responsiveness to changing requirements. However, in many industries, especially those subject to regulatory frameworks and compliance standards, Agile practices can present unique challenges related to meeting legal requirements and ensuring adherence to regulations. This section explores the compliance and regulatory challenges faced by Agile teams and strategies to address them.

*Regulatory Considerations in Agile*

1. **Data Privacy Regulations**: Regulations like the General Data Protection Regulation (GDPR) and the Health Insurance Portability and Accountability Act (HIPAA) impose strict requirements on the handling of personal and sensitive data. Agile teams must ensure that their software complies with data privacy laws.

2. **Financial Regulations**: In the finance and banking sector, there are extensive regulations regarding the handling of financial data, reporting, and security. Agile teams working on financial software must navigate these regulations to avoid legal issues.

3. **Healthcare Compliance**: Agile teams developing healthcare applications must adhere to regulations like the Health Insurance Portability and Accountability Act (HIPAA) in the United States. Ensuring patient data security and privacy is paramount.

4. **Pharmaceutical and Life Sciences**: Companies in the pharmaceutical and life sciences industries must comply with stringent regulations from organizations like the U.S. Food and Drug Administration (FDA). Agile teams developing software for these industries face the challenge of aligning with regulatory requirements.

*Compliance Challenges in Agile*

1. **Changing Requirements**: Agile's emphasis on adaptability and responding to change can make it challenging to document and maintain traceability of requirements, which is often required for compliance audits.

2. **Documentation**: Regulatory compliance often demands extensive documentation, such as design specifications, test plans, and validation records. Agile's preference

for working software over comprehensive documentation can conflict with these requirements.

3.  **Risk Management**: Agile teams need to identify and mitigate risks effectively. Regulatory compliance often includes specific risk management processes and documentation that may differ from Agile practices.

4.  **Audits and Traceability**: Compliance audits may require extensive traceability of requirements, code changes, and test results. Agile teams must establish processes and tools to maintain audit trails.



1.  **Cross-Functional Collaboration**: Foster collaboration between compliance experts, legal teams, and Agile practitioners. Encourage open communication to ensure that compliance requirements are understood and integrated into Agile processes.

2.  **Compliance Backlogs**: Create a compliance backlog to track and prioritize compliance-related tasks, such as documentation updates, risk assessments, and compliance testing.

3.  **Automated Testing**: Implement automated testing and continuous integration to ensure that compliance-related tests are executed consistently and that documentation is automatically generated.

4.  **Documentation as Code**: Treat documentation as code by using version control systems to manage compliance-related documents. This allows for traceability and change management.

5.  **Compliance by Design**: Integrate compliance considerations into the design and development process from the beginning, rather than addressing them as an afterthought.

6.  **Regulatory Expertise**: Employ experts in regulatory compliance or seek external consultants who can provide guidance on interpreting and meeting regulatory requirements.

7.  **Training and Education**: Ensure that Agile team members are educated on compliance requirements relevant to their projects.

In conclusion, Agile development can coexist with compliance and regulatory requirements with proper planning and alignment. Agile teams should prioritize understanding and addressing compliance challenges to avoid legal issues and maintain the trust of stakeholders in regulated industries. While Agile's adaptability is a strength, it should be balanced with the need for careful documentation and adherence to regulatory standards.

# Section 12.5: Data Security and Privacy in Scrum

Data security and privacy have become paramount concerns in today's digital landscape. Agile teams, including Scrum teams, must take proactive measures to protect sensitive data and ensure compliance with privacy regulations. This section explores the importance of data security and privacy in Scrum and provides guidelines for safeguarding data throughout the development process.

*The Significance of Data Security and Privacy*

1. **Trust and Reputation**: Data breaches can severely damage an organization's reputation and erode customer trust. Scrum teams must prioritize data security to maintain trust with stakeholders.

2. **Legal and Regulatory Compliance**: Many regions have stringent data protection laws, such as GDPR in Europe and CCPA in California. Agile teams must ensure that their processes align with these regulations to avoid legal consequences.

3. **Data Breach Costs**: Data breaches can result in significant financial losses due to fines, legal fees, and compensation to affected parties. Investing in data security is often more cost-effective than dealing with a breach.

4. **Client Expectations**: Clients and customers expect their data to be handled securely and privately. Failure to meet these expectations can lead to lost business opportunities.

*Integrating Data Security and Privacy in Scrum*

1. **Security by Design**: Implement security and privacy considerations from the start of the project. Include threat modeling and risk assessments in sprint planning to identify potential vulnerabilities.

2. **User Story Refinement**: During backlog refinement, include security and privacy requirements as part of user story acceptance criteria. This ensures that security is not an afterthought.

3. **Secure Coding Practices**: Train development teams in secure coding practices to mitigate common vulnerabilities, such as injection attacks, authentication issues, and data exposure.

4. **Automated Security Testing**: Integrate automated security testing into the continuous integration (CI) pipeline. Tools like static code analysis and dynamic application security testing (DAST) can help identify vulnerabilities early.

5. **Data Classification**: Classify data based on sensitivity and regulatory requirements. Ensure that access controls and encryption mechanisms are appropriate for the data's classification.

6. **Privacy Impact Assessments**: Conduct privacy impact assessments (PIAs) to identify and mitigate privacy risks associated with data processing activities. PIAs are particularly important when handling personal data.

7. **User Consent**: Implement mechanisms for obtaining user consent when collecting and processing personal data. Ensure transparency in data handling practices.

8. **Data Minimization**: Collect and retain only the data necessary for the intended purpose. Minimizing data reduces the risk associated with data breaches.

9. **Incident Response Plan**: Develop an incident response plan that outlines the steps to take in case of a data breach. Scrum teams should be aware of their roles in incident management.

10. **Security Training**: Provide ongoing security awareness training for all team members to keep them informed about emerging threats and best practices.

11. **External Assessments**: Consider external security assessments, penetration testing, and audits to validate the security and privacy controls in place.

12. **Documentation and Traceability**: Maintain documentation of security and privacy measures implemented during the project. This documentation helps demonstrate compliance during audits.

13. **Data Retention and Deletion**: Define data retention policies and procedures, including secure data disposal methods when data is no longer needed.

In conclusion, data security and privacy are integral aspects of software development, and Scrum teams must actively address them throughout the project lifecycle. By embedding security and privacy practices into the Scrum framework, teams can build trust with stakeholders, mitigate risks, and ensure compliance with legal and regulatory requirements. This proactive approach is essential for protecting sensitive data and maintaining the integrity of the development process.

---

## Chapter 13: Remote Scrum Teams

### Section 13.1: Setting Up for Remote Success

The rise of remote work has led to a significant shift in how Scrum teams operate. While the Scrum framework remains the same, adapting it to the remote environment comes with its own set of challenges and opportunities. In this section, we will explore how to set up remote Scrum teams for success.

#### The Advantages of Remote Scrum Teams

1. **Access to Global Talent**: Remote work allows Scrum teams to tap into a global talent pool, enabling them to work with the best professionals regardless of their location.

2. **Improved Work-Life Balance**: Team members often report better work-life balance when working remotely, which can lead to increased job satisfaction and productivity.

3. **Cost Savings**: Remote work can lead to cost savings for both organizations and individuals, as it reduces the need for physical office space and commuting expenses.

4. **Flexibility**: Remote Scrum teams can offer more flexible working hours, accommodating team members in different time zones.



1. **Communication Tools**: Invest in reliable communication and collaboration tools. Video conferencing, chat applications, and project management software are essential for remote teams.

2. **Clear Expectations**: Set clear expectations for remote team members regarding working hours, availability, and communication protocols.

3. **Time Zone Management**: If the team spans multiple time zones, establish a common time window for meetings and collaboration, and rotate meeting times to ensure fairness.

4. **Documentation**: Emphasize the importance of documentation. Remote teams rely heavily on written communication to ensure everyone is on the same page.

5. **Regular Check-Ins**: Schedule regular check-in meetings, such as daily stand-ups and sprint reviews, to maintain team cohesion and transparency.

6. **Remote-Friendly Tools**: Choose tools and processes that are remote-friendly. For example, use digital whiteboards and online retrospectives.

7. **Security and Data Privacy**: Ensure that remote work does not compromise data security or privacy. Implement secure access and data handling practices.

8. **Team Building**: Plan virtual team-building activities to foster a sense of belonging and camaraderie among team members.

9. **Professional Development**: Support remote team members' professional development by providing access to online training and resources.



1. **Isolation**: Remote team members may experience feelings of isolation and disconnection. Regular social interactions and team-building activities can help address this challenge.

2. **Communication Barriers**: Miscommunication can occur more easily in remote settings. Encourage open and clear communication, and address issues promptly.

3. **Time Zone Differences**: Coordinating across different time zones can be challenging. Agile practices, such as asynchronous communication and distributed decision-making, can help.

4. **Distractions**: Remote team members may face distractions at home. Encourage them to create dedicated workspaces and set boundaries.

5. **Overworking**: Some remote team members struggle to disconnect from work. Encourage a healthy work-life balance.

In conclusion, setting up remote Scrum teams for success requires careful planning and consideration of the unique challenges and advantages of remote work. By providing the right tools, clear expectations, and support for team members, organizations can leverage the benefits of remote work while maintaining the efficiency and effectiveness of Scrum practices.

---

## Section 13.2: Tools and Techniques for Remote Collaboration

Remote Scrum teams rely on a variety of tools and techniques to collaborate effectively despite physical distance. In this section, we'll explore the essential tools and practices that facilitate seamless collaboration among remote team members.

### Communication Tools

1. **Video Conferencing**: Platforms like Zoom, Microsoft Teams, or Google Meet enable face-to-face communication, fostering a sense of connection among team members.

2. **Chat and Messaging Apps**: Tools like Slack, Microsoft Teams, or Slack offer real-time chat and file-sharing capabilities, making it easy to ask questions and share updates.

3. **Email**: While often considered traditional, email remains a vital tool for asynchronous communication, especially for sharing detailed information or documentation.

4. **Project Management Software**: Tools like Jira, Trello, or Asana help Scrum teams manage their backlogs, sprint planning, and task assignments effectively.

5. **Documentation Platforms**: Platforms like Confluence or Microsoft SharePoint allow teams to create and collaborate on documentation, keeping everyone on the same page.

### Virtual Whiteboards and Collaboration Spaces

1. **Miro**: Miro is a popular online whiteboard platform that allows teams to brainstorm, create diagrams, and work on visual planning together in real time.

2. **Microsoft Whiteboard**: Integrated with Microsoft Teams, this tool provides a virtual canvas for ideation and collaboration.

3. **Jamboard**: Google's digital whiteboard, Jamboard, offers a collaborative space for drawing, adding sticky notes, and brainstorming.

### Screen Sharing and Remote Control

1. **Screen Sharing**: Team members can use screen-sharing features in video conferencing tools to present their work, facilitate discussions, or troubleshoot issues.

2. **Remote Control**: In some cases, remote control functionality allows team members to take control of each other's computers to provide assistance or demonstrate tasks.

### Agile Practices for Remote Teams

1. **Asynchronous Communication**: Recognize that team members may work in different time zones. Encourage asynchronous communication by using chat messages, emails, or project management tools.

2. **Daily Stand-ups**: Conduct daily stand-up meetings via video conferencing to provide updates, share progress, and identify impediments.

3. **Sprint Reviews**: Remote sprint reviews can be conducted effectively using video conferencing. Share the sprint's accomplishments with stakeholders.

4. **Retrospectives**: Hold remote retrospectives using collaboration tools like Miro or digital retrospectives platforms designed for remote teams.

5. **Pair Programming and Mob Programming**: Even remotely, team members can collaborate on coding tasks through screen sharing and pair programming.

### Security and Privacy

1. **Secure Connections**: Ensure that all communication and collaboration tools are accessed through secure, encrypted connections to protect sensitive information.

2. **Access Controls**: Implement strict access controls to ensure that only authorized individuals can access critical documents and systems.

3. **Data Handling**: Train team members on proper data handling procedures to prevent data breaches or leaks.

4. **Privacy Regulations**: Be aware of and compliant with data privacy regulations relevant to your region and industry.

In summary, remote Scrum teams can thrive with the right combination of communication tools, collaboration platforms, and agile practices. By embracing these tools and techniques, remote teams can maintain productivity, transparency, and effective collaboration, regardless of their geographical locations.

Building and sustaining a positive team culture is crucial for the success of remote Scrum teams. While physical distance may pose challenges, it's possible to foster a strong sense of community and collaboration among team members. In this section, we'll explore strategies to create and maintain a healthy remote team culture.

### Define Team Values and Norms

1. **Shared Values**: Start by defining the team's core values. What principles guide your work? Values like transparency, trust, and respect are often crucial in remote settings.

2. **Team Norms**: Establish clear norms for communication, meetings, and work hours. Having agreed-upon norms ensures that everyone understands expectations.

### Effective Communication

1. **Regular Updates**: Encourage team members to provide regular status updates. Daily stand-up meetings and weekly progress reports can help maintain transparency.

2. **Open Channels**: Create open channels for communication where team members can discuss both work-related and non-work topics. This fosters social connections.

3. **Video Conferencing**: Whenever possible, use video conferencing for meetings. Seeing faces and body language helps build a stronger connection than just audio.

### Virtual Team Building Activities

1. **Icebreakers**: Start meetings with icebreakers or team-building games to promote bonding and reduce the feeling of isolation.

2. **Virtual Coffee Breaks**: Organize virtual coffee breaks or informal chats where team members can discuss non-work topics.

3. **Celebrations**: Celebrate birthdays, work anniversaries, or project milestones virtually. Small gestures can have a big impact.

### Recognition and Appreciation

1. **Recognition**: Acknowledge and appreciate team members' efforts. Publicly recognize their achievements during meetings or through dedicated channels.

2. **Feedback**: Encourage constructive feedback, both positive and negative. Feedback helps team members grow and improves team dynamics.

1. **Inclusivity**: Ensure that all team members feel included and valued. Be mindful of different time zones, cultures, and backgrounds.

2. **Diversity**: Embrace diversity in your team. Diverse teams bring varied perspectives and ideas, contributing to innovation.



1. **Continuous Learning**: Support team members' professional growth. Offer training opportunities and encourage certifications related to their roles.

2. **Knowledge Sharing**: Create a culture of knowledge sharing. Encourage team members to share insights, articles, or new tools they discover.



1. **Well-being Initiatives**: Promote well-being initiatives. Provide resources on managing stress, maintaining work-life balance, and seeking help when needed.

2. **Flexible Hours**: Allow flexibility in work hours to accommodate personal needs and family responsibilities.



1. **Early Intervention**: Address conflicts promptly. Encourage open and respectful dialogue to resolve issues.

2. **Mediation**: In cases of escalated conflicts, consider involving a neutral mediator to facilitate resolution.



1. **Trust Your Team**: Trust is the foundation of remote work. Trust your team members to complete their tasks and contribute effectively.

2. **Autonomy**: Empower team members with autonomy in how they approach their work. Autonomy boosts motivation and creativity.



1. **Team Wins**: Celebrate team wins and achievements. Whether it's a successful sprint or the release of a new feature, recognize and celebrate together.

2. **Personal Milestones**: Acknowledge personal milestones like marriages, births, or significant life events.

In summary, building and sustaining a remote team culture requires deliberate effort and a commitment to fostering a sense of belonging and collaboration. By defining values, promoting effective communication, and embracing inclusivity, remote Scrum teams can create a positive and thriving team culture that transcends physical boundaries.

Managing time zones is a common challenge for remote Scrum teams, especially when team members are spread across different regions of the world. Time zone differences can lead to scheduling conflicts, delayed responses, and potential productivity issues. However, with effective strategies, these challenges can be mitigated. In this section, we'll explore time zone challenges and solutions for remote Scrum teams.

### Time Zone Challenges

1. **Scheduling Meetings**: Finding suitable meeting times that accommodate team members in various time zones can be a logistical puzzle. Some team members might have to attend meetings very early or late in their day.

2. **Communication Delays**: Waiting for responses or clarifications from team members in different time zones can slow down project progress, especially when quick decisions are needed.

3. **Overlap Hours**: The limited overlap hours between team members' workdays can affect real-time collaboration and hinder the resolution of urgent issues.

4. **Sprint Planning**: Coordinating sprint planning, reviews, and retrospectives when team members are in different time zones can be challenging.

### Solutions to Time Zone Challenges

1. **Implement a Global Time Zone Policy**: Define a standard time zone that the team uses for scheduling meetings and planning. This reduces confusion and simplifies coordination.

2. **Use Time Zone Converters**: Provide team members with access to time zone conversion tools or apps that help them easily convert meeting times to their local time.

3. **Rotate Meeting Times**: Rotate meeting times to ensure that the burden of early or late meetings is shared among team members. This promotes fairness and avoids consistently disadvantaging certain team members.

4. **Record Meetings**: Whenever possible, record important meetings, such as sprint planning and reviews, so that team members who couldn't attend in real-time can catch up later.

5. **Asynchronous Communication**: Encourage asynchronous communication, especially for non-urgent matters. Use tools like email, chat, or collaboration platforms where team members can respond when it's convenient for them.

6. **Overlap Hours**: Identify the overlap hours when most team members are available. Schedule important meetings or discussions during these hours to maximize real-time collaboration.

7. **Use Visual Schedules**: Create visual schedules that display team members' working hours and availability. This helps in understanding when it's appropriate to reach out to someone.

8. **Adapt Sprint Length**: Adjust the length of sprints to accommodate time zone differences. For example, consider longer sprints if team members need more time for collaboration due to limited overlap hours.

9. **Empower Teams**: Empower smaller, cross-functional sub-teams to work independently on specific tasks or user stories. This reduces the need for constant real-time collaboration.

10. **Time Zone Awareness**: Develop a culture of time zone awareness within the team. Encourage team members to be mindful of each other's working hours and commitments.

11. **Documentation**: Emphasize the importance of thorough documentation. Ensure that all decisions, discussions, and action items are well-documented and accessible to all team members.

12. **Time Zone-Friendly Tools**: Choose collaboration tools that offer features designed to address time zone challenges. Some tools offer built-in time zone conversion features and availability indicators.

13. **Regular Check-Ins**: Conduct regular check-ins with team members in different time zones to understand their unique challenges and gather feedback on how to improve collaboration.

In conclusion, managing time zone challenges in remote Scrum teams requires a combination of clear policies, effective communication, and flexibility. By acknowledging the diversity of time zones and implementing these solutions, remote teams can maintain productivity, enhance collaboration, and ensure that time zone differences don't become barriers to success.

---

## Section 13.5: Remote Team Building Activities

Building a strong and cohesive remote Scrum team is essential for successful project delivery. Remote work can sometimes lead to feelings of isolation and disconnection among team members. To overcome this challenge, Scrum Masters and team leaders can organize remote team building activities that foster collaboration, boost morale, and create a sense of belonging. In this section, we'll explore various remote team building activities that can help remote Scrum teams bond and work together effectively.

Remote team building is not just about having fun; it's a strategic approach to enhancing team dynamics and performance. Here are some reasons why it's important:

1. **Building Trust**: Team building activities help team members get to know each other on a personal level, which fosters trust and rapport.

2. **Communication**: They improve communication skills, ensuring that team members can effectively convey their thoughts and ideas, even in a remote setting.

3. **Motivation**: Team building activities can boost motivation and morale, leading to increased engagement and productivity.

4. **Problem Solving**: Many activities require collaboration and problem-solving, which can improve teamwork and decision-making skills.

5. **Reducing Isolation**: Remote work can be isolating. Team building activities create a sense of connection and reduce feelings of isolation.

## Remote Team Building Activities

1. **Virtual Icebreakers**: Start meetings with fun icebreaker questions or activities to encourage interaction and engagement.

2. **Online Games**: Host online games or trivia contests that team members can participate in during breaks or after work hours.

3. **Themed Meetings**: Organize themed meetings where team members dress up or decorate their virtual backgrounds according to a chosen theme.

4. **Show-and-Tell Sessions**: Allow team members to share something interesting from their remote work environment during meetings.

5. **Virtual Coffee Breaks**: Set up informal virtual coffee breaks or happy hours for team members to socialize.

6. **Collaborative Playlist**: Create a collaborative music playlist where team members add their favorite songs.

7. **Book Club**: Start a virtual book club where team members read and discuss a book together.

8. **Mentorship Program**: Pair experienced team members with newer ones for mentorship and knowledge sharing.

9. **Online Workshops**: Host online workshops or training sessions on relevant topics to enhance skills and knowledge.

10. **Escape Room Challenges**: Participate in virtual escape room challenges that require problem-solving and teamwork.

11. **Fitness Challenges**: Encourage team members to participate in fitness challenges or step competitions.

12. **Virtual Lunches**: Schedule virtual team lunches where everyone eats together and chats about non-work topics.

13. **Recognition and Awards**: Create virtual awards and recognition ceremonies to celebrate achievements and contributions.

14. **Online Hackathons**: Organize virtual hackathons or innovation challenges to spur creativity.

15. **Remote Retreats**: Plan virtual team retreats with team-building exercises, workshops, and relaxation activities.

16. **Trivia Nights**: Host trivia nights with various categories to test team members' knowledge.

17. **Photo Contests**: Run photo contests around specific themes or subjects.

18. **Collaborative Art**: Engage in collaborative art projects where team members contribute to a shared piece of artwork.

19. **Online Puzzles**: Solve online puzzles or riddles together as a team.

20. **Storytelling Sessions**: Have storytelling sessions where team members share interesting or funny anecdotes.

It's important to choose team building activities that align with your team's interests and preferences. Additionally, consider the cultural and time zone diversity within your team when scheduling these activities to ensure that all team members can participate comfortably.

Incorporating remote team building activities into your Scrum practices can lead to a more connected and motivated team, ultimately improving the overall performance and satisfaction of remote Scrum team members.

# Chapter 14: Scrum in Complex Projects

## Section 14.1: Handling Large and Complex Projects with Scrum

Handling large and complex projects with Scrum can be a challenging yet rewarding endeavor. Scrum, originally designed for small teams working on relatively simple projects, has evolved to accommodate complex projects by introducing various scaling frameworks and best practices. In this section, we'll explore the strategies and techniques for successfully applying Scrum in large and complex project environments.

### The Challenge of Complexity

Complex projects are characterized by their intricate nature, involving numerous variables, dependencies, and uncertainties. These projects often span extended durations and involve cross-functional teams, making them challenging to manage using traditional project management approaches.

The Scrum framework, with its iterative and incremental approach, provides a strong foundation for addressing complexity. However, adapting Scrum to large and complex projects requires careful planning and customization.

### Scaling Scrum

One of the primary approaches to handling complex projects with Scrum is scaling. Scaling Scrum involves extending the Scrum framework to multiple teams working together on a single project. Several frameworks, such as the Scaled Agile Framework (SAFe), Large Scale Scrum (LeSS), and Disciplined Agile Delivery (DAD), offer guidance on how to scale Scrum effectively.

#### SAFe (Scaled Agile Framework)

SAFe is one of the most popular scaling frameworks for Scrum. It provides a structured approach to scaling Scrum practices to large enterprises. SAFe introduces roles, ceremonies, and artifacts that align multiple Agile Release Trains (ARTs) toward a common business and technical goal. It includes principles, practices, and a governance model that helps organizations coordinate the work of multiple Scrum teams.

#### LeSS (Large Scale Scrum)

LeSS takes a minimalistic approach to scaling Scrum. It emphasizes simplicity and focuses on the fundamental principles of Scrum. LeSS is based on the idea that scaling should not add unnecessary complexity. Instead, it encourages organizations to keep Scrum as simple as possible while coordinating the efforts of multiple Scrum teams.

#### DAD (Disciplined Agile Delivery)

DAD is a process decision framework that extends Scrum by providing additional guidance on various aspects of project delivery. DAD acknowledges that one size does not fit all and offers a range of lifecycle and delivery options. It allows organizations to tailor their approach to suit the specific needs of complex projects.

### Coordination and Collaboration

In complex projects, coordination and collaboration among teams become critical. Effective communication channels, cross-team ceremonies, and a shared understanding of project goals are essential. Scrum of Scrums, a technique where representatives from each Scrum team meet to discuss dependencies and challenges, can be beneficial.

### Backlog Management

Managing a single Product Backlog becomes challenging as projects grow in complexity. Prioritizing and decomposing backlog items, along with continuous refinement, are essential to ensure that teams are working on the most valuable tasks. Tools and techniques for backlog management, such as Value Stream Mapping and Impact Mapping, can be valuable in complex projects.

### Risk Management

Complex projects inherently involve higher levels of risk. Identifying and managing risks should be an ongoing process. Scrum provides transparency through its artifacts, such as the Sprint Backlog and Increment, which can help teams identify risks early. Risk mitigation strategies should be part of the project's planning and execution.

### Continuous Improvement

Complex projects are an opportunity for continuous improvement. Regular retrospectives and the inspection and adaptation principle of Scrum are even more critical in complex environments. Teams should be encouraged to experiment with process improvements and adapt to changing circumstances.

### Conclusion

Handling large and complex projects with Scrum requires a combination of scaling frameworks, effective coordination, and a commitment to Agile principles. While it presents challenges, Scrum's adaptability and iterative nature make it a viable approach for managing even the most complex endeavors. Successful application of Scrum in complex projects can result in improved project outcomes, higher quality deliverables, and increased customer satisfaction.

---

## Section 14.2: Risk Management in Agile Projects

Agile methodologies, including Scrum, are known for their flexibility and adaptability, which make them suitable for managing complex and dynamic projects. However, with this flexibility comes the need for effective risk management. In this section, we will explore the principles and practices of risk management in Agile projects, particularly focusing on Scrum.



Agile risk management differs from traditional project risk management in several ways. Traditional methods often involve creating a detailed risk management plan upfront and addressing risks based on this plan. In Agile, risk management is more iterative and integrated into the ongoing project work.

Here are key principles of Agile risk management:

1. **Continuous Identification:** Agile teams continuously identify and assess risks throughout the project. This includes both known risks and those that emerge as the project progresses.

2. **Prioritization:** Risks are prioritized based on their potential impact on project goals and objectives. High-priority risks are addressed first.

3. **Adaptive Response:** Agile teams respond to risks in an adaptive manner, adjusting plans and strategies as needed. This might involve changing the scope, reprioritizing work, or seeking stakeholder input.

4. **Transparency:** Agile promotes transparency, making risks visible to the team and stakeholders. This fosters open communication and collaboration in risk mitigation.

## Risk Management Activities in Scrum

In Scrum, risk management is an integral part of the framework. Here are some key activities and practices related to risk management in Scrum:

### 1. Sprint Planning

During Sprint Planning, the Scrum Team discusses potential risks that might affect the Sprint's goal. Identifying these risks early allows the team to plan for mitigations or contingencies.

### 2. Daily Stand-ups

The Daily Stand-up meetings provide a platform for team members to raise any concerns or risks they encounter while working on Sprint tasks. This early detection allows for quick responses.

### 3. Sprint Review

The Sprint Review includes inspecting the Increment and gathering feedback from stakeholders. This can reveal risks related to product quality or stakeholder expectations, which can be addressed in subsequent Sprints.

The Sprint Retrospective is an opportunity for the team to reflect on their processes and identify improvements. If risks have impacted the Sprint, the team can discuss ways to prevent similar issues in the future.

*5. Product Backlog Refinement*

As the Product Backlog is continuously refined, the team may identify risks related to incomplete or ambiguous backlog items. These can be clarified or addressed with the Product Owner.

*6. Risk Burndown Charts*

Similar to the traditional Burndown Chart that tracks work progress, Agile teams can use Risk Burndown Charts to track the progress of risk mitigation efforts. This visual representation helps teams monitor the status of identified risks.

## Agile Risk Mitigation Strategies

In Agile, the approach to risk mitigation emphasizes early action and flexibility. Some common risk mitigation strategies in Agile projects include:

- **Iterative Development:** Agile projects break work into small increments, allowing teams to address risks incrementally and make adjustments as needed.
- **Prototyping:** Building prototypes or proofs of concept early can help identify technical or design risks before they become major issues.
- **Regular Inspection and Adaptation:** Frequent inspection of work and adaptation to changing circumstances is key to managing risks effectively.
- **Customer Feedback:** Agile encourages regular feedback from customers and stakeholders, helping to identify and address risks related to product expectations.

## Conclusion

Agile risk management in Scrum is a dynamic and collaborative process that focuses on early identification, prioritization, and adaptive response to risks. By integrating risk management into the Agile framework, teams can effectively navigate uncertainty and deliver valuable outcomes even in complex and evolving project environments.

---

## Section 14.3: Integrating Scrum with Other Project Management Approaches

In some organizations or project environments, Scrum may not be the sole project management approach in use. It's common to find hybrid scenarios where Scrum is integrated with other methodologies or frameworks to meet specific project needs. This section explores the integration of Scrum with other project management approaches and highlights the benefits and challenges of such combinations.



Several reasons drive the integration of Scrum with other project management approaches:

1.  **Regulatory Requirements:** In industries with strict regulatory compliance requirements, such as healthcare or finance, Scrum alone may not provide sufficient documentation or control. Organizations often integrate Scrum with traditional project management to ensure compliance.

2.  **Large-Scale Projects:** Complex projects involving multiple Scrum Teams may benefit from integrating Scrum with scaled Agile frameworks like SAFe (Scaled Agile Framework) or LeSS (Large Scale Scrum). These frameworks offer guidance on coordinating efforts across teams.

3.  **Legacy Systems:** Organizations with legacy systems may find it challenging to fully embrace Agile development. In such cases, Scrum can be integrated with Waterfall or other methodologies to manage legacy components.

## Benefits of Integration

### 1. Flexibility

Integrating Scrum with other approaches provides flexibility. Teams can choose the best practices from each methodology to suit the project's unique needs. For example, Scrum can handle product development, while traditional project management is used for regulatory compliance.

### 2. Risk Management

Combining Scrum's adaptive approach with traditional project management's risk management processes allows organizations to manage risks effectively. Risks can be identified and mitigated using traditional methods, while Scrum focuses on delivering value.

### 3. Scalability

Large organizations can scale Agile practices effectively by integrating Scrum with scaled Agile frameworks. This allows for better coordination among multiple Scrum Teams while maintaining alignment with the organization's goals.

## Challenges of Integration

### 1. Communication

Effective communication between teams following different methodologies can be challenging. Misalignment in terminology and processes may lead to misunderstandings and delays.

Scrum and traditional project management often have different organizational cultures. Bridging these cultural gaps requires time and effort.

*3. Complexity*

Integration can add complexity to project management. Teams must carefully plan and manage the integration process to avoid introducing unnecessary overhead.

### Examples of Integration

1. **Scrum and PRINCE2:** PRINCE2 (Projects IN Controlled Environments) is a structured project management framework. Organizations often integrate Scrum with PRINCE2 to combine Scrum's iterative development with PRINCE2's governance and control.

2. **Scrum and Waterfall:** In situations where a legacy system is involved, Scrum can be used for new development, while Waterfall is applied for maintaining and integrating with the legacy system.

3. **SAFe and Scrum:** Large enterprises might adopt the Scaled Agile Framework (SAFe) at the portfolio, program, or team level. SAFe incorporates Scrum practices within a larger framework, allowing organizations to scale Agile across multiple teams.

### Best Practices for Integration

Successful integration of Scrum with other approaches requires careful planning and execution. Here are some best practices to consider:

- **Clearly Define Roles and Responsibilities:** Ensure that everyone understands their roles and responsibilities within the integrated environment.

- **Common Language:** Establish a common language and terminology that all teams can understand and use.

- **Regular Communication:** Promote regular communication and collaboration between teams to address challenges and concerns promptly.

- **Evaluate Progress:** Continuously evaluate the integration's effectiveness and make adjustments as necessary.

- **Training and Education:** Provide training and education to team members to ensure they are familiar with both Scrum and the integrated approach.

### Conclusion

Integrating Scrum with other project management approaches can be a practical solution to meet specific project requirements. However, it's essential to approach integration thoughtfully, considering the benefits and challenges, and to tailor the integrated approach to the organization's needs. When done successfully, integration can allow organizations to harness the strengths of both Agile and traditional project management to achieve project success.

---

## Section 14.4: Multi-Team Coordination and Dependency Management

In large and complex projects, coordinating multiple Scrum Teams becomes a crucial aspect of project management. Each Scrum Team operates independently but often needs to work collaboratively to deliver a valuable product. Multi-team coordination and dependency management are vital for the success of such projects.

### Challenges in Multi-Team Environments

#### 1. Cross-Team Dependencies

When different Scrum Teams are working on related features or components, dependencies naturally arise. For example, one team may need the output of another team to complete their work. Managing these dependencies is critical to avoid delays and ensure smooth progress.

#### 2. Communication

Effective communication between teams is essential for multi-team coordination. Miscommunication or lack of communication can lead to misunderstandings and hinder progress.

#### 3. Scaling Scrum

As the number of Scrum Teams increases, it becomes challenging to maintain alignment with Agile principles and practices. Scaling frameworks like SAFe or LeSS offer guidance on how to coordinate multiple teams effectively.

### Strategies for Multi-Team Coordination

#### 1. Scrum of Scrums

The Scrum of Scrums is a technique used to facilitate communication and coordination between multiple Scrum Teams. In this approach, representatives from each team meet regularly to discuss progress, identify dependencies, and address any impediments. It ensures that teams are aligned and working toward a common goal.

#### 2. Dependency Backlogs

Creating a dependency backlog can help teams manage and prioritize cross-team dependencies. Each dependency is documented, and teams work together to resolve them efficiently. The backlog ensures transparency and accountability.

*3. Cross-Team Collaboration*

Encouraging cross-team collaboration fosters a culture of teamwork and collective ownership. Teams can hold joint review sessions, share best practices, and collaborate on challenging problems. This approach promotes knowledge sharing and reduces dependencies.

*4. Co-Locating Teams*

When feasible, co-locating Scrum Teams in the same physical or virtual space can enhance communication and coordination. Proximity makes it easier for teams to interact and resolve issues promptly.

## Scaling Frameworks

Several scaling frameworks provide guidance on coordinating multiple Scrum Teams. Here are two popular ones:

*1. SAFe (Scaled Agile Framework)*

SAFe offers a comprehensive framework for large-scale Agile transformations. It includes roles, ceremonies, and artifacts that help organizations coordinate multiple teams while ensuring alignment with business goals. SAFe supports various levels of scaling, from team-level to portfolio-level.

*2. LeSS (Large Scale Scrum)*

LeSS is a framework that extends Scrum principles to large-scale environments. It emphasizes simplicity and transparency and suggests that scaling is achieved by having fewer roles and artifacts compared to other frameworks. LeSS maintains Scrum's core practices while providing guidelines for multiple-team coordination.

## Tools for Multi-Team Coordination

Various tools can aid in multi-team coordination and dependency management. These tools help teams visualize dependencies, track progress, and communicate effectively. Some common tools include Jira, Rally, VersionOne, and Azure DevOps.

## Conclusion

Multi-team coordination and dependency management are critical aspects of large-scale Agile projects. While Scrum provides the foundation for team-level Agile practices, organizations must implement strategies, frameworks, and tools to coordinate multiple teams successfully. Effective coordination ensures that dependencies are managed efficiently, communication is clear, and project goals are met on time. By adopting the right practices and scaling frameworks, organizations can navigate the complexities of multi-team environments and deliver value to their customers.

In the world of Agile and Scrum, complex projects often present unique challenges that require innovative solutions. Real-world case studies provide valuable insights into how organizations have tackled complexity using Scrum principles and practices. Let's explore some case studies of complex Scrum projects.

### Case Study 1: Large-Scale Software Migration

**Challenge:** A multinational corporation needed to migrate its legacy software systems to modern cloud-based solutions. The complexity lay in the sheer size and scale of the software landscape, with numerous interconnected applications.

**Solution:** The organization adopted SAFe (Scaled Agile Framework) to coordinate multiple Scrum Teams. They established a Program Increment (PI) planning cadence to align teams' efforts. Each team focused on migrating specific modules or applications. Regular Scrum of Scrums meetings ensured cross-team collaboration. Continuous integration and automated testing reduced deployment risks.

**Outcome:** By leveraging SAFe's principles and practices, the organization successfully migrated its software landscape to the cloud within the planned timeline. The project improved system reliability, reduced maintenance costs, and enhanced user experience.

### Case Study 2: Hardware and Software Integration

**Challenge:** An aerospace company faced the challenge of integrating complex hardware components with specialized software for a new aircraft. The project involved multiple suppliers and intricate dependencies.

**Solution:** The organization adopted LeSS (Large Scale Scrum) to simplify the coordination process. They established cross-functional Scrum Teams that included hardware and software engineers, testers, and domain experts. Daily stand-ups and frequent review meetings facilitated collaboration. Dependency management boards visualized and tracked hardware-software dependencies.

**Outcome:** Using LeSS, the organization successfully integrated hardware and software components. The aircraft passed rigorous testing and certification processes, meeting safety and performance standards. The project was delivered on time, reducing development costs.

### Case Study 3: Regulatory Compliance in Healthcare

**Challenge:** A healthcare software company needed to ensure its products complied with evolving regulatory requirements in various countries. Navigating changing regulations while maintaining product development velocity was a significant challenge.

**Solution:** The company implemented a hybrid approach, combining Scrum with Kanban. Scrum Teams focused on feature development, while Kanban boards managed regulatory compliance tasks. The teams regularly reviewed compliance requirements during sprint reviews. Frequent communication with regulatory experts ensured alignment.

**Outcome:** The hybrid approach enabled the company to meet regulatory deadlines without compromising on feature development. Products remained compliant, reducing legal risks. The organization demonstrated adaptability and responsiveness to regulatory changes.

### Case Study 4: Agile Transformation in a Financial Institution

**Challenge:** A large financial institution sought to transform its traditional project management practices to Agile methodologies. The challenge was not only in changing processes but also in shifting the organization's culture.

**Solution:** The institution embarked on an Agile transformation journey, starting with pilot Scrum Teams. They invested in comprehensive training for teams and leaders. Agile Coaches provided guidance and support. Continuous improvement initiatives, such as retrospectives, were integral to the process.

**Outcome:** Over time, the institution underwent a successful Agile transformation. Scrum became the standard project management approach, improving project visibility and customer satisfaction. The culture shift towards Agile values and principles contributed to long-term success.

### Case Study 5: E-commerce Platform Scalability

**Challenge:** An e-commerce company experienced rapid growth and needed to scale its platform to handle increased traffic and demand during peak seasons.

**Solution:** The organization embraced Agile principles across the board. Scrum Teams focused on optimizing platform performance and scalability. Regular backlog grooming sessions prioritized performance-related user stories. Automated testing and performance monitoring were integrated into the development process.

**Outcome:** By adopting Agile practices and Scrum, the e-commerce company improved platform scalability and reliability. The platform successfully handled peak-season traffic, resulting in increased revenue and customer satisfaction.

These case studies demonstrate that Agile and Scrum can be adapted to address the complexities of various industries and project types. The key lies in choosing the right framework, practices, and approaches to align with the project's specific challenges and goals. Through effective implementation and continuous improvement, organizations can navigate complex projects successfully while delivering value to their stakeholders.

# Chapter 15: Continuous Improvement and Innovation

## Section 15.1: Fostering a Culture of Innovation

In today's rapidly evolving business landscape, organizations must foster a culture of innovation to stay competitive and adapt to changing market dynamics. This culture of innovation is equally vital in Agile and Scrum environments, where continuous improvement is a core principle. In this section, we explore strategies for fostering a culture of innovation within Scrum teams and organizations.

### Embracing the Agile Mindset

Innovation begins with adopting the Agile mindset. Scrum teams and their members should be open to change, experimentation, and the idea that there is always room for improvement. The Agile Manifesto's values and principles encourage individuals and interactions over processes and tools, customer collaboration, and responding to change. Embracing these principles creates an environment where innovation thrives.

### Psychological Safety

Psychological safety is the foundation of innovation. Team members must feel safe to express their ideas, take risks, and make mistakes without fear of judgment or retribution. Leaders and Scrum Masters play a crucial role in creating psychological safety within their teams. Regular retrospectives provide a platform for team members to voice their concerns, share insights, and suggest improvements.

### Cross-Functional Collaboration

Innovation often occurs at the intersection of different disciplines. Scrum teams should consist of cross-functional members who bring diverse skills and perspectives to the table. Encouraging collaboration between team members with varied backgrounds fosters creativity and innovation. Product Owners, developers, designers, and testers should work closely together to generate innovative solutions.

### Encouraging Experimentation

Innovation involves experimentation. Scrum teams should be encouraged to try out new approaches, technologies, or processes to solve problems and improve their work. Experimentation might lead to failures, but these failures can be valuable learning experiences. Teams should celebrate both successes and failures as they represent opportunities for growth and innovation.

### User-Centric Design

Innovation should be driven by a deep understanding of user needs and preferences. Scrum teams should prioritize user-centric design practices, such as user research, usability testing, and feedback loops with customers. The goal is to create products and features that genuinely address user pain points and provide value.

In the midst of sprint cycles and daily work, it's essential to allocate dedicated time for innovation. Some organizations implement practices like "Innovation Fridays" or "Hackathons," where team members can work on innovative projects unrelated to their regular tasks. This dedicated time allows for creative thinking and experimentation without disrupting the sprint's rhythm.

## Continuous Learning

A culture of innovation thrives on continuous learning. Scrum teams and individuals should be encouraged to expand their knowledge and skill sets. This can involve attending conferences, taking online courses, or participating in communities of practice. Learning from others' experiences and staying up-to-date with industry trends can inspire innovative ideas.

## Celebrating Innovation

Celebrating and recognizing innovative contributions is essential. Teams should acknowledge and reward innovative ideas and solutions. This recognition can take the form of awards, peer recognition, or even small tokens of appreciation. Celebrating innovation reinforces its value within the organization.

In conclusion, fostering a culture of innovation within Scrum teams and organizations is vital for staying competitive and continuously improving. It requires embracing the Agile mindset, creating psychological safety, promoting cross-functional collaboration, encouraging experimentation, prioritizing user-centric design, dedicating time for innovation, promoting continuous learning, and celebrating innovative contributions. When these elements come together, teams and organizations can innovate and thrive in an ever-changing business landscape.

---

## Section 15.2: Techniques for Continuous Improvement

Continuous improvement is a fundamental aspect of Agile and Scrum methodologies. It involves regularly assessing processes, practices, and outcomes to identify areas for enhancement and striving for incremental progress. In this section, we delve into various techniques that Scrum teams and organizations can employ to facilitate continuous improvement.

## Retrospectives

Retrospectives are a cornerstone of continuous improvement in Scrum. These regular meetings, typically held at the end of each sprint, provide a safe space for teams to reflect on their performance. During retrospectives, team members discuss what went well, what could have been better, and what actions can be taken to improve in the upcoming sprint.

The retrospective format encourages open dialogue and the identification of concrete action items for positive change.

## Kaizen

Kaizen, a Japanese term for "continuous improvement," emphasizes the importance of small, incremental changes over time. Scrum teams can adopt Kaizen principles by focusing on making minor process improvements on a daily basis. These improvements can be as simple as refining communication practices, optimizing workflows, or automating repetitive tasks. Over time, these small changes accumulate and lead to significant improvements in efficiency and effectiveness.

## Lean Thinking

Lean thinking, derived from Lean manufacturing principles, promotes the elimination of waste and the optimization of processes. Scrum teams can apply Lean principles by identifying and reducing activities that do not add value to the product or customer. This can involve streamlining workflows, reducing waiting times, and minimizing unnecessary documentation. Lean thinking encourages teams to focus on delivering value while eliminating non-value-added activities.

## 5 Whys

The "5 Whys" technique is a problem-solving approach used to identify the root cause of issues or obstacles. Scrum teams can utilize this technique during retrospectives or when facing challenges. By repeatedly asking "why" and digging deeper into the causes of a problem, teams can uncover underlying issues and address them more effectively. This approach promotes a deeper understanding of problems and prevents surface-level fixes.

## Lean Six Sigma

Lean Six Sigma combines Lean principles with statistical methods to achieve process improvement and waste reduction. While it may be more commonly associated with traditional project management, elements of Lean Six Sigma can be integrated into Scrum practices. Analyzing data, measuring process performance, and using statistical tools can help identify areas for improvement and guide data-driven decision-making.

## Value Stream Mapping

Value stream mapping is a visual tool used to analyze and optimize the flow of work in a process. Scrum teams can create value stream maps to identify bottlenecks, delays, and areas of inefficiency in their workflow. By visualizing the end-to-end process, teams can make informed decisions about where to focus improvement efforts. Value stream mapping is particularly valuable for understanding how work moves through various stages and identifying opportunities for streamlining.

In product development, A/B testing involves comparing two versions of a feature or design to determine which one performs better with users. Scrum teams can use A/B testing to continuously improve their products or services. By collecting data on user interactions and preferences, teams can make informed decisions about which features to enhance or modify. A/B testing allows teams to iterate on designs and functionalities based on real user feedback.

## Root Cause Analysis

Root cause analysis is a structured method for identifying the underlying causes of problems or failures. Scrum teams can employ techniques like the "5 Whys" or cause-and-effect diagrams (Ishikawa or fishbone diagrams) to conduct root cause analysis. This approach helps teams go beyond addressing symptoms and target the fundamental issues contributing to challenges. Identifying root causes is crucial for implementing effective and lasting solutions.

In conclusion, continuous improvement is at the heart of Agile and Scrum methodologies. Scrum teams and organizations can employ various techniques to foster a culture of continuous improvement. Retrospectives, Kaizen, Lean thinking, the 5 Whys, Lean Six Sigma, value stream mapping, A/B testing, and root cause analysis are valuable tools and practices that enable teams to identify opportunities for enhancement and make iterative progress toward delivering greater value to customers.

---

## Section 15.3: Experimentation and Learning in Scrum

In the world of Agile and Scrum, the ability to experiment and learn from those experiments is crucial for teams and organizations to stay competitive and innovative. This section explores the significance of experimentation and how it can be integrated into Scrum practices.

### The Importance of Experimentation

Experimentation is the process of trying out new ideas, approaches, or solutions to gain insights and learn from the outcomes. In the context of Scrum, experimentation is valuable for several reasons:

1. **Innovation**: Experimentation fosters innovation by encouraging teams to think outside the box and explore novel solutions to problems.

2. **Continuous Improvement**: It aligns with the Agile principle of continuous improvement by providing opportunities to refine processes and practices.

3. **Risk Mitigation**: Experimentation allows teams to assess risks and uncertainties in a controlled environment before committing to a full-scale implementation.

4. **Customer-Centricity**: It helps teams better understand customer needs and preferences through iterative testing and feedback gathering.



To incorporate experimentation into Scrum, consider the following practices:

### 1. Hypothesis-Driven Development

Hypothesis-driven development involves formulating hypotheses about how a change or feature will impact the product and then testing those hypotheses. Teams can create user stories based on hypotheses and prioritize them accordingly. After implementation, data and user feedback are collected to validate or refute the hypotheses.

### 2. Sprint Goals

In each sprint, teams can set specific goals related to experimentation. These goals might involve improving user engagement, increasing conversion rates, or enhancing product usability. Sprints can be structured to include time for experimentation alongside regular development work.

### 3. A/B Testing

A/B testing, as mentioned in the previous section, is a powerful experimentation technique. Scrum teams can implement A/B tests to compare different versions of a feature or design and measure their impact on user behavior. This data-driven approach helps teams make informed decisions about which variations are more effective.

### 4. Prototyping

Prototyping involves creating lightweight, functional models of features or interfaces to gather user feedback. Scrum teams can use prototypes to validate design concepts and identify potential issues early in the development process. Rapid prototyping allows for quick iterations based on user input.

### 5. Cross-Functional Collaboration

Experimentation often requires input from various team members with different skills and perspectives. Cross-functional collaboration within Scrum teams can enhance the quality and diversity of experiments. Developers, designers, product owners, and other stakeholders can contribute their expertise to formulate hypotheses and design experiments.

Retrospectives, a standard Scrum practice, provide an opportunity to reflect on the outcomes of experiments. Teams can discuss what was learned, whether hypotheses were validated, and how to apply those learnings in future sprints.

### Challenges and Considerations

While experimentation is valuable, it comes with challenges:

- **Resource Allocation**: Experimentation requires time and resources, which must be balanced with regular development work.

- **Data Collection**: Gathering meaningful data and feedback can be challenging, and teams need the right tools and processes in place.

- **Risk Management**: Teams must carefully manage risks associated with experiments, especially when they impact critical aspects of the product.

- **Communication**: Effective communication is crucial to ensure that everyone on the team understands the purpose and results of experiments.

In conclusion, experimentation is an essential component of Scrum that encourages innovation, continuous improvement, and customer-centricity. By incorporating practices like hypothesis-driven development, A/B testing, prototyping, and cross-functional collaboration, Scrum teams can leverage experimentation to drive product excellence and adapt to changing market conditions.

---

## Section 15.4: Encouraging Creativity in Teams

Creativity is a driving force behind innovation and problem-solving. In Scrum, fostering creativity within your team can lead to more effective solutions and a more engaging work environment. This section explores strategies and techniques for encouraging creativity in Scrum teams.

### The Role of Creativity in Scrum

Creativity is not limited to artistic endeavors; it plays a vital role in problem-solving and generating innovative solutions. In the context of Scrum, creativity is essential for the following reasons:

1. **Problem-Solving**: Scrum teams often face complex problems that require creative thinking to solve. Creative solutions can lead to better outcomes and improved products.

2. **Adaptation**: In the fast-paced world of Scrum, creative teams are more adaptable. They can quickly adjust to changing circumstances and find new ways to achieve their goals.

3. **Engagement**: Fostering creativity can make work more engaging and enjoyable for team members, which can boost morale and productivity.

4. **Innovation**: Creativity is the foundation of innovation. Scrum teams that embrace creativity are more likely to come up with groundbreaking ideas and stay competitive.

## Strategies for Encouraging Creativity

Here are strategies that Scrum Masters and team members can use to encourage creativity within their teams:

### 1. Create a Safe Environment

Teams must feel safe to express their creative ideas without fear of criticism or judgment. Establish a culture of psychological safety where team members can share their thoughts openly.

### 2. Diverse Teams

Diversity in teams can lead to a broader range of perspectives and ideas. Embrace diversity in terms of skills, backgrounds, and experiences to stimulate creativity.

### 3. Set Aside Time for Creativity

Incorporate dedicated time for brainstorming and creative thinking into your Scrum events, such as Sprint Planning and Retrospectives.

### 4. Encourage Curiosity

Foster a sense of curiosity among team members. Encourage them to ask questions, explore new concepts, and seek innovative solutions.

### 5. Embrace Failure

Innovation often involves trial and error. Encourage the team to view failures as learning opportunities and not as negative outcomes.

### 6. Provide Tools and Resources

Equip your team with the tools, software, and resources they need to experiment and explore creative ideas.

### 7. Cross-Disciplinary Collaboration

Encourage team members from different roles to collaborate. Cross-disciplinary collaboration can lead to unique solutions.

Use creativity-enhancing techniques such as mind mapping, brainstorming sessions, or design thinking workshops to generate ideas.

*9. Support Autonomy*

Give team members the autonomy to make decisions and explore creative solutions within the boundaries of the project.

*10. Celebrate Creativity*

Recognize and celebrate creative contributions within the team. Acknowledging and rewarding creative efforts can motivate team members to continue innovating.

## Challenges in Fostering Creativity

While fostering creativity is essential, it can also present challenges:

- **Resistance to Change**: Some team members may resist creative approaches if they are accustomed to traditional methods.

- **Time Constraints**: The fast pace of Scrum can make it challenging to allocate time for creative activities.

- **Conflict Management**: Creative teams may encounter conflicts related to differing ideas and opinions. Effective conflict resolution is crucial.

- **Balancing Creativity and Delivery**: Striking a balance between creativity and meeting project deadlines is essential.

In conclusion, creativity is a valuable asset in Scrum that can lead to better problem-solving, innovation, and team engagement. Scrum Masters and team members should actively promote creativity within their teams by creating a safe environment, embracing diversity, setting aside time for creative activities, and providing the necessary resources and support. While challenges may arise, the benefits of encouraging creativity far outweigh the difficulties.

---

## Section 15.5: Measuring and Rewarding Innovation

Innovation is a driving force behind progress and success in the business world. Scrum teams that foster a culture of innovation often find themselves at the forefront of their industries. However, measuring and rewarding innovation can be a challenge. In this section, we'll explore how Scrum teams can effectively measure and reward innovative efforts.

Measuring innovation is essential for several reasons:

1. **Assessment**: It allows organizations to assess the impact of innovative ideas and initiatives on their products, services, or processes.

2. **Improvement**: Measurement helps identify areas where innovation can be improved or optimized.

3. **Accountability**: It holds teams and individuals accountable for contributing to innovation.

4. **Recognition**: Measuring innovation provides a basis for recognizing and rewarding innovative contributions.

## Key Metrics for Measuring Innovation

1. **Ideation Rate**: This metric measures the number of innovative ideas generated within a given period. It provides insight into the team's creativity and ideation process.

2. **Implementation Rate**: Tracking how many innovative ideas are implemented and become part of the product or process is crucial. This metric indicates the team's ability to execute on innovative concepts.

3. **Impact Metrics**: Assess the impact of innovation on key performance indicators (KPIs) such as revenue, customer satisfaction, or operational efficiency. Quantifying the effects of innovation is essential for demonstrating its value.

4. **Experimentation Success Rate**: Measure the success rate of experiments conducted to test innovative hypotheses. This metric reflects the team's ability to validate and refine innovative ideas.

5. **Time to Market**: How quickly innovative ideas are transformed into tangible outcomes, such as new features or products, is a crucial metric. Shortening the time to market can be a competitive advantage.

6. **Customer Feedback**: Collect and analyze customer feedback related to innovative changes. Positive feedback indicates successful innovation that meets customer needs.

## Rewarding Innovation

Rewarding innovation is an important aspect of promoting a culture of creativity and continuous improvement. Here are some strategies for rewarding innovative efforts in Scrum teams:

1. **Recognition and Appreciation**: Publicly recognize and appreciate team members who contribute innovative ideas or solutions. Simple gestures like shout-outs during Sprint Reviews or team meetings can go a long way.

2. **Innovation Awards**: Establish innovation awards or recognition programs within the organization. These awards can be given to individuals or teams that make significant contributions to innovation.

3. **Incentives**: Consider offering financial incentives or bonuses for outstanding innovations. This can provide tangible rewards for innovative efforts.

4. **Career Development**: Provide opportunities for career advancement or additional responsibilities to team members who consistently drive innovation.

5. **Training and Development**: Invest in training and development programs that support innovation. Offering courses or workshops in creative thinking, design thinking, or problem-solving can empower team members to be more innovative.

6. **Innovation Time**: Dedicate a portion of team's time to work on innovative projects or ideas of their choice. Google's famous "20% time" is an example of this approach.

7. **Innovation Days or Hackathons**: Organize innovation days or hackathons where teams can collaborate on innovative projects outside their regular work.

8. **Innovation Metrics**: Tie performance evaluations and promotions to innovative contributions, as measured by the innovation metrics mentioned earlier.

## Challenges in Measuring and Rewarding Innovation

Measuring and rewarding innovation comes with its challenges:

- **Subjectivity**: Innovation can be subjective, and different people may have varying opinions on what constitutes innovation.

- **Fear of Failure**: Teams may be hesitant to innovate if they fear failure or negative consequences. Creating a safe environment is crucial in overcoming this challenge.

- **Short-Term vs. Long-Term Impact**: Balancing short-term and long-term innovation can be tricky. Organizations must consider the potential long-term benefits of innovation, even if they don't yield immediate results.

- **Tracking and Documentation**: Measuring innovation requires effective tracking and documentation, which can be time-consuming.

In conclusion, measuring and rewarding innovation is vital for Scrum teams aiming to stay competitive and drive continuous improvement. Key metrics can help evaluate the impact of innovation, while recognition, incentives, and career development opportunities can motivate teams to innovate. Overcoming challenges related to subjectivity, fear of failure, and tracking is essential in building a culture of innovation within Scrum teams and organizations.

Conflict is an inevitable aspect of any team dynamic, and in the context of Scrum, it's essential to address conflicts early to maintain a healthy and productive work environment. Conflicts can arise from various sources, including differences in opinions, misunderstandings, or competing priorities. As a Scrum Master, part of your role is to identify and mitigate conflicts proactively. Here are some key strategies to identify and address conflicts at an early stage:

1. **Active Listening**: Effective conflict resolution begins with active listening. When team members express concerns or disagreements, listen attentively to understand their perspective fully. Encourage team members to share their thoughts and feelings openly.

2. **Regular Check-Ins**: Conduct regular one-on-one and team check-ins to create a safe space for team members to voice their concerns. These check-ins provide an opportunity for team members to discuss any issues they might be facing.

3. **Observe Team Interactions**: Pay close attention to team interactions during meetings, stand-ups, and collaborative sessions. Look for signs of tension, frustration, or non-verbal cues that may indicate underlying conflicts.

4. **Encourage Open Communication**: Foster an environment of open and transparent communication within the team. Encourage team members to express their opinions and concerns without fear of judgment or reprisal.

5. **Conflict Resolution Frameworks**: Familiarize yourself with conflict resolution frameworks such as the Thomas-Kilmann Conflict Mode Instrument (TKI). This tool can help you and your team members understand your conflict resolution styles and find common ground.

6. **Mediation Skills**: Develop mediation skills to facilitate discussions between conflicting parties. Act as a neutral mediator to help team members reach a resolution collaboratively.

7. **Address Root Causes**: When conflicts arise, dig deeper to identify the root causes rather than just addressing surface-level issues. Understanding the underlying reasons for conflicts can lead to more effective resolutions.

8. **Define Team Norms**: Establish clear team norms and guidelines for communication and conflict resolution. Team members should be aware of the expected behavior when conflicts arise.

9. **Conflict Logs**: Maintain a conflict log to document and track conflicts as they occur. Include information about the nature of the conflict, parties involved, resolutions proposed, and outcomes.

10. **Feedback Loops**: Implement feedback loops to gather input from team members on a regular basis. This can help identify recurring issues and areas where conflicts tend to arise.

11. **Training and Workshops**: Offer conflict resolution training and workshops for team members to equip them with the necessary skills to handle conflicts constructively.

12. **Escalation Path**: Establish an escalation path for conflicts that cannot be resolved within the team. Ensure that there is a clear process for involving higher management or stakeholders when needed.

By identifying and addressing conflicts early, you can create a more harmonious and productive Scrum team. Conflict resolution is not about avoiding disagreements but about managing them in a way that fosters collaboration and growth within the team.

---

## Section 16.2: Negotiation Skills for Scrum Masters

Negotiation is a crucial skill for a Scrum Master, as it plays a significant role in resolving conflicts, prioritizing work, and achieving consensus within the Scrum team. Scrum Masters often find themselves in situations where negotiation is required, whether it's in backlog prioritization meetings, resolving resource conflicts, or managing stakeholder expectations. Here are some essential negotiation skills and strategies that Scrum Masters can employ:

1. **Effective Communication**: Effective negotiation begins with clear and open communication. Ensure that all parties involved understand the issues at hand, and encourage them to express their perspectives and needs.

2. **Active Listening**: Listen actively to the concerns, interests, and objectives of all parties. Pay attention not only to what is said but also to the emotions and underlying motivations behind their positions.

3. **Empathy**: Show empathy towards the concerns and viewpoints of others. Understand their emotions and try to put yourself in their shoes to see the situation from their perspective.

4. **Identify Common Ground**: Look for areas of agreement and common interests among the parties involved. Identifying shared objectives can serve as a foundation for negotiation.

5.  **Explore Options**: Brainstorm potential solutions collaboratively. Encourage creative thinking and alternative approaches to address the issues at hand.

6.  **Prioritize Interests Over Positions**: Instead of focusing solely on the positions of each party, explore their underlying interests. This can often lead to more creative and mutually beneficial solutions.

7.  **Maintain Neutrality**: As a Scrum Master, it's crucial to maintain a neutral stance in negotiations. Avoid taking sides or showing bias, and focus on facilitating the process rather than advocating for a particular outcome.

8.  **Stay Calm Under Pressure**: Negotiations can sometimes become heated or emotional. It's essential for the Scrum Master to remain calm and composed, serving as a stabilizing influence.

9.  **Establish Clear Agreements**: Ensure that any agreements or resolutions reached during negotiations are clear, specific, and documented. This helps prevent misunderstandings later on.

10. **Manage Expectations**: Set realistic expectations for all parties involved. If certain requests or demands cannot be met, communicate this clearly and explain the reasons behind it.

11. **Use Objective Criteria**: Whenever possible, base decisions on objective criteria rather than subjective opinions. This can lend credibility to the negotiation process.

12. **Practice Patience**: Negotiations can take time, especially when dealing with complex issues or multiple parties. Be patient and persistent in seeking mutually beneficial solutions.

13. **Know When to Seek Help**: In some cases, negotiations may reach an impasse, or conflicts may be beyond the scope of the Scrum Master's role. In such situations, don't hesitate to involve higher management or stakeholders for assistance.

14. **Continuous Learning**: Improve your negotiation skills through continuous learning and self-improvement. Attend workshops, read books, and seek feedback to enhance your abilities in this area.

15. **Feedback and Reflection**: After negotiations, reflect on the process and outcomes. Solicit feedback from the involved parties to understand what worked well and where improvements can be made.

Negotiation is not about winning or losing but about finding mutually beneficial solutions that enable the Scrum team to move forward effectively. By honing their negotiation skills, Scrum Masters can contribute to a more collaborative and harmonious work environment, where conflicts are resolved, and team members are aligned toward common goals.

As a Scrum Master, one of your key roles is to facilitate and promote a collaborative and productive work environment within your Scrum team. However, conflicts and disputes can arise, even in the most harmonious teams. In such cases, the Scrum Master can employ mediation techniques to help team members resolve their differences and restore a positive working atmosphere. Mediation is a structured and impartial process aimed at finding mutually acceptable solutions to disputes. Here are some mediation techniques that can be valuable for Scrum Masters:

1. **Active Listening**: Begin by actively listening to the concerns and perspectives of the parties involved. Encourage them to express themselves fully without interruption. This helps them feel heard and valued.

2. **Neutral Ground**: Find a neutral and private space where the mediation can take place. Ensure that all parties feel comfortable and safe to express their thoughts and emotions.

3. **Establish Ground Rules**: Set clear ground rules for the mediation session. These rules should include guidelines for respectful communication, allowing each party to speak, and refraining from personal attacks.

4. **Encourage Empathy**: Ask each party to try and understand the other's perspective. This can be achieved by asking questions like, "How do you think the other person feels about this situation?" and "What do you think their intentions were?"

5. **Define the Issues**: Help the parties clarify the specific issues at the heart of the dispute. Often, conflicts can become tangled with multiple concerns, so breaking them down into manageable components is essential.

6. **Stay Neutral**: As the mediator, it's crucial to remain neutral and not take sides. Your role is to facilitate the process, not to advocate for one party's position.

7. **Encourage Collaboration**: Emphasize the importance of finding a mutually acceptable solution. Encourage the parties to work together to brainstorm potential solutions.

8. **Brainstorm Solutions**: Facilitate a brainstorming session where both parties can suggest possible solutions to the issues. Encourage creative thinking and be open to all ideas, even if they seem unconventional.

9. **Evaluate and Prioritize**: After generating a list of potential solutions, evaluate each one based on its feasibility and potential impact. Prioritize the solutions that are most likely to resolve the dispute.

10. **Agreement and Commitment**: Once a mutually acceptable solution is identified, ensure that both parties agree to it. Ask them to commit to implementing the solution and to hold each other accountable.

11. **Follow-Up**: After the mediation session, follow up with the parties to ensure that the agreed-upon solution is being implemented and that the dispute has been effectively resolved.

12. **Confidentiality**: Stress the importance of confidentiality. What is discussed during the mediation session should remain confidential, fostering trust among team members.

13. **Continuous Improvement**: Use the mediation process as an opportunity for continuous improvement. Reflect on the effectiveness of the mediation and seek feedback from the parties involved.

14. **Seek Professional Help**: In cases where disputes are deeply ingrained or highly emotional, it may be necessary to seek the assistance of a professional mediator or conflict resolution expert.

Mediation can be a powerful tool for Scrum Masters to help teams resolve conflicts and maintain a positive and productive working environment. By following these techniques and principles, Scrum Masters can play a pivotal role in ensuring that team members collaborate effectively and that disputes are addressed constructively.

---

## Section 16.4: Maintaining Team Harmony

Maintaining harmony within a Scrum team is a critical responsibility for a Scrum Master. A harmonious team is more likely to be productive, creative, and motivated, leading to the successful delivery of high-quality products. In this section, we will explore various strategies and practices that Scrum Masters can employ to foster and maintain team harmony.

### 1. Build Trust

Trust is the foundation of any successful team. Scrum Masters should work to establish trust among team members by being transparent, reliable, and consistent in their actions. Encourage open and honest communication, and lead by example in demonstrating trustworthiness.

### 2. Effective Communication

Clear and effective communication is key to preventing misunderstandings and conflicts within the team. Ensure that team members understand their roles, responsibilities, and goals. Encourage active listening and provide opportunities for team members to express their thoughts and concerns.

### 3. Conflict Resolution

Conflicts are inevitable in any team, but how they are handled can greatly impact team harmony. Scrum Masters should be skilled in conflict resolution techniques and should address conflicts promptly and constructively. Encourage team members to address issues openly and respectfully.

### 4. Foster Collaboration

Promote a culture of collaboration where team members feel comfortable sharing ideas and working together. Encourage cross-functional collaboration and emphasize the importance of collective ownership of the product and the process.

### 5. Recognition and Appreciation

Recognize and appreciate the contributions of team members. Celebrate achievements, both big and small, and publicly acknowledge the efforts of individuals. This fosters a positive atmosphere and motivates team members to continue performing at their best.

### 6. Empowerment

Empower team members by giving them autonomy and decision-making authority within their areas of expertise. Empowered team members are more engaged and motivated to take ownership of their work.

### 7. Regular Feedback

Provide regular feedback to team members, both in the form of constructive criticism and positive reinforcement. Feedback should be specific, actionable, and focused on improvement.

### 8. Maintain a Healthy Work-Life Balance

Team harmony can be negatively affected when team members are stressed or overworked. Ensure that team members have a healthy work-life balance and encourage them to take breaks and vacations when needed.

### 9. Professional Development

Support the professional development of team members by providing opportunities for learning and growth. This can include training, workshops, and mentoring. When team members feel that their career development is supported, they are more likely to remain engaged and committed to the team.

## 10. Celebrate Diversity

Embrace the diversity of your team members and encourage an inclusive environment where everyone's perspectives are valued. A diverse team can bring fresh ideas and creativity to the table.

## 11. Lead by Example

Scrum Masters should lead by example when it comes to behaviors and attitudes. Demonstrating professionalism, respect, and a commitment to the Scrum values sets a positive tone for the team.

## 12. Team Building Activities

Organize team-building activities and events to strengthen the bonds among team members. These activities can be both fun and educational, fostering camaraderie and collaboration.

## 13. Continuous Improvement

Regularly assess team dynamics and performance to identify areas for improvement. Encourage retrospectives and use the feedback to make necessary adjustments to processes and team interactions.

## 14. Conflict Prevention

Preventing conflicts before they escalate is often more effective than resolving them after the fact. Monitor team interactions, identify potential sources of conflict, and address them proactively.

Maintaining team harmony is an ongoing process that requires vigilance, empathy, and dedication. Scrum Masters who prioritize team well-being and foster a positive working environment are more likely to see their teams flourish and deliver exceptional results. Remember that team harmony is not a static state but a dynamic one that requires continuous attention and care.

---

## Section 16.5: Case Studies: Conflict Resolution in Scrum Teams

In the world of Scrum, conflicts within teams can arise due to various reasons, including differences in opinions, miscommunication, or external pressures. In this section, we'll explore real-world case studies that highlight how Scrum Masters and teams have successfully managed and resolved conflicts to maintain team harmony and productivity.

In one Scrum team, two team members had conflicting personalities that led to frequent disagreements. The Scrum Master recognized the issue and facilitated a one-on-one conversation with each team member separately to understand their perspectives. Through active listening and empathy, the Scrum Master helped both individuals see the value in their differences and how their complementary skills could benefit the team. They agreed to communicate more openly and respectfully, which improved collaboration within the team.



Another Scrum team faced conflicts because team members had different priorities for the product backlog items. This resulted in delays and confusion during sprint planning. The Scrum Master introduced a backlog refinement session where the Product Owner and team members discussed and clarified priorities. Additionally, the team started using the "Dot Voting" technique to collectively decide on the most important backlog items. This approach ensured that everyone's perspectives were considered, and it improved the team's focus and alignment.



A Scrum team was working under intense external pressure to deliver a critical project. This pressure led to stress and frustration among team members. The Scrum Master recognized the signs of burnout and organized a team-building activity to relieve stress and boost morale. They also engaged with stakeholders to negotiate more realistic deadlines and expectations. By addressing both internal and external pressures, the team regained its composure and productivity.



In a large organization transitioning to Agile, teams were using different Agile frameworks and practices, causing confusion and conflicts. The Scrum Master initiated a cross-team discussion to align on common Agile practices and principles. They created a shared document that documented the agreed-upon practices and ensured consistent implementation across teams. This effort reduced conflicts and improved the overall Agile transformation.



A Scrum team disagreed on whether to address technical debt immediately or focus solely on delivering new features. The Scrum Master facilitated a discussion where team members shared their concerns and considered the long-term consequences of ignoring technical debt. Ultimately, the team agreed to allocate a small portion of each sprint to address technical debt, ensuring a balance between feature development and maintaining a healthy codebase.

Conflicts sometimes arise between Scrum teams and external stakeholders with different expectations. The Scrum Master acted as a mediator, organizing meetings with stakeholders to clarify requirements and priorities. They emphasized the importance of transparency and regular feedback. This approach helped build trust and fostered better collaboration between the teams and stakeholders.

These case studies illustrate the importance of proactive conflict resolution and the role of the Scrum Master in facilitating communication and collaboration within Scrum teams. Conflict is not inherently negative; when managed effectively, it can lead to improved team dynamics and better outcomes. Scrum Masters should embrace conflict resolution as an essential skill in their toolkit, ensuring that teams can work harmoniously and deliver value consistently.

# Chapter 17: The Future of Scrum and Agile

## Section 17.1: Emerging Trends in Agile and Scrum

The Agile and Scrum methodologies have evolved significantly since their inception. In this section, we will explore the emerging trends and developments that are shaping the future of Agile and Scrum.

### 1. Beyond Software Development

Traditionally, Agile and Scrum were predominantly associated with software development. However, one of the emerging trends is the expansion of Agile principles and practices into other domains. Agile is being adopted in marketing, manufacturing, education, and even non-profit organizations. This diversification highlights the universal applicability of Agile principles beyond software.

### 2. Agile at Scale

As organizations increasingly adopt Agile and Scrum, there is a growing demand for scaling Agile practices across larger enterprises. Frameworks like SAFe (Scaled Agile Framework), LeSS (Large Scale Scrum), and Spotify Model are gaining popularity. These frameworks provide guidance on how to implement Agile principles at scale, enabling organizations to manage complex projects and products more effectively.

### 3. DevOps Integration

The integration of DevOps with Agile and Scrum is becoming more prevalent. DevOps focuses on automating the software delivery pipeline, enhancing collaboration between development and operations teams, and achieving continuous delivery. Combining Agile, Scrum, and DevOps practices streamlines the entire software development process, from idea to production, resulting in faster and more reliable releases.

### 4. Agile for Remote Work

The COVID-19 pandemic accelerated the adoption of remote work practices. Agile teams had to adapt to remote collaboration, and this trend is likely to continue. Agile tooling and practices are evolving to better support remote work, with an emphasis on asynchronous communication, virtual retrospectives, and improved online collaboration tools.

### 5. Data-Driven Decision Making

Agile teams are increasingly using data to make informed decisions. Agile metrics and analytics are being leveraged to track progress, identify bottlenecks, and forecast project outcomes. Data-driven decision making enhances transparency and enables teams to continuously improve their processes.

## 6. Agile Leadership

Leadership in Agile organizations is undergoing a transformation. Agile leaders are expected to embody the Agile mindset, foster a culture of trust and empowerment, and provide servant leadership. Leadership development programs are focusing on equipping leaders with the skills required to support Agile teams effectively.

## 7. Agility in Governance and Compliance

Even in highly regulated industries, there is a move towards agility in governance and compliance. Agile methods are being applied to ensure that regulatory requirements are met while still maintaining the flexibility to respond to changing customer needs.

## 8. AI and Automation

Artificial intelligence (AI) and automation are being integrated into Agile practices to enhance efficiency and productivity. AI-powered tools are assisting with backlog prioritization, test automation, and even predictive analysis to identify potential project risks.

## 9. Sustainability and Agile

Sustainability considerations, including environmental and social responsibility, are gaining importance in Agile practices. Agile teams are encouraged to factor sustainability into their decision-making processes, aligning with broader corporate social responsibility goals.

In conclusion, Agile and Scrum continue to evolve and adapt to the changing landscape of business and technology. These emerging trends reflect the resilience and versatility of Agile methodologies, which remain at the forefront of delivering value to organizations across various industries. As Agile continues to mature, it will likely play a crucial role in shaping the future of work and innovation.

---

## Section 17.2: The Evolving Role of the Scrum Master

The role of the Scrum Master has been pivotal in the success of Agile and Scrum teams. As Agile practices continue to evolve, the responsibilities and expectations associated with the Scrum Master role are also changing. In this section, we will delve into the evolving role of the Scrum Master and the skills required to excel in this position.

## 1. Beyond Ceremonial Facilitation

Traditionally, Scrum Masters were often seen as facilitators of Scrum ceremonies, ensuring that meetings like sprint planning, daily stand-ups, and retrospectives ran smoothly. While these facilitation skills remain important, the role has expanded far beyond that. Scrum

Masters are now expected to be coaches, mentors, and change agents who guide teams in becoming self-organized and continuously improving.



## 2. Servant Leadership

The concept of servant leadership, which has always been a core aspect of the Scrum Master role, is gaining even more prominence. Scrum Masters are expected to serve the team by removing impediments, protecting the team from external distractions, and enabling the team to make decisions autonomously. This approach fosters a culture of trust and collaboration within the team.

## 3. Coach and Mentor

Scrum Masters are increasingly taking on the roles of coaches and mentors. They help team members develop their skills, improve their Agile practices, and overcome challenges. Effective coaching involves asking powerful questions, actively listening, and providing constructive feedback. Scrum Masters also guide product owners and stakeholders in understanding their roles within the Scrum framework.

## 4. Change Agent

As organizations embrace Agile at a larger scale, Scrum Masters are often at the forefront of driving change. They advocate for Agile principles and practices within the organization, educate stakeholders about the benefits of Agile, and work to eliminate organizational impediments that hinder Agile adoption. Their role extends to influencing the organization's culture and processes.

## 5. Collaboration and Communication

Effective communication and collaboration skills are essential for Scrum Masters. They must facilitate open and transparent communication within the team and with stakeholders. Scrum Masters often bridge the gap between technical and non-technical stakeholders, ensuring a common understanding of project goals and progress.

## 6. Conflict Resolution

Conflict is inevitable in any team, and Scrum Masters are responsible for addressing conflicts early and constructively. They use their mediation skills to facilitate discussions and find resolutions that benefit the team. Scrum Masters create a safe space for team members to express concerns and work towards solutions.

## 7. Continuous Learning

The Agile landscape is constantly evolving, with new practices and frameworks emerging. Scrum Masters must commit to continuous learning and self-improvement. Staying updated on the latest Agile trends and techniques is crucial for adapting to changing circumstances and providing valuable guidance to teams.

Scrum Masters are increasingly using metrics and data to gain insights into team performance and project progress. They leverage Agile metrics such as velocity, cycle time, and burndown charts to identify areas for improvement and make informed decisions.

### 9. Empowering Teams

Ultimately, the evolving role of the Scrum Master centers around empowering teams to become self-organized, self-managing, and highly effective. Scrum Masters enable teams to take ownership of their work, make decisions collectively, and continuously improve their processes.

In conclusion, the role of the Scrum Master is evolving from a ceremonial facilitator to a multi-faceted leader, coach, and change agent. Scrum Masters play a critical role in fostering Agile principles and practices within organizations, empowering teams, and driving continuous improvement. As the Agile landscape continues to evolve, Scrum Masters will remain at the forefront of Agile transformation, helping organizations adapt to the changing demands of the modern business environment.

---

## Section 17.3: New Tools and Technologies for Scrum Teams

The world of Agile and Scrum is dynamic, and as it continues to evolve, so do the tools and technologies that support Scrum teams in their daily work. In this section, we'll explore some of the new tools and technologies that are making waves in the world of Scrum and Agile development.

### 1. Scrum Software Platforms

Scrum teams rely on software platforms to streamline their work processes. While established tools like Jira, Trello, and Asana continue to be popular choices, new and specialized Scrum tools have emerged. These platforms offer features specifically designed for Agile and Scrum practices, such as sprint planning, backlog management, burndown charts, and retrospectives. Some platforms even integrate machine learning and AI to provide predictive analytics for better decision-making.

### 2. Collaboration and Communication Tools

Effective communication and collaboration are at the core of Agile methodologies. Tools like Slack, Microsoft Teams, and Discord have become essential for Scrum teams, enabling real-time chat, video conferencing, file sharing, and integration with other Scrum software. These tools help remote and distributed teams stay connected and work seamlessly.

### 3. Test Automation Frameworks

Automation is a key practice in Agile and Scrum, and test automation is no exception. New test automation frameworks and tools, such as Cypress, TestCafe, and Playwright, have gained popularity for their simplicity and effectiveness. They allow Scrum teams to automate testing processes, resulting in faster feedback and higher-quality software.

### 4. Continuous Integration and Continuous Delivery (CI/CD) Pipelines

CI/CD pipelines have become indispensable for Agile development. Tools like Jenkins, GitLab CI/CD, and CircleCI enable Scrum teams to automate building, testing, and deploying software. CI/CD pipelines help teams achieve rapid and reliable releases, reducing the time between code changes and production deployment.

### 5. DevOps Practices

DevOps practices have become closely aligned with Agile and Scrum. Tools like Docker, Kubernetes, and Ansible facilitate containerization, orchestration, and automation of infrastructure and deployment processes. Scrum teams embrace DevOps principles to ensure that development and operations work seamlessly together.

### 6. Kanban Boards

While Kanban is a separate Agile framework, it's often used in conjunction with Scrum, especially for visualizing work and managing flow. Digital Kanban board tools like Kanbanize, LeanKit, and Trello offer customizable boards for tracking work items, setting WIP (Work in Progress) limits, and visualizing the flow of tasks.

### 7. Artificial Intelligence and Machine Learning

AI and ML are finding applications in Agile and Scrum, particularly in areas like sprint forecasting, anomaly detection, and automated quality assurance. Teams use AI-powered tools to predict sprint outcomes, identify patterns in development data, and detect potential issues early in the development process.

### 8. Virtual Reality (VR) and Augmented Reality (AR)

While still emerging, VR and AR technologies are beginning to impact Agile and Scrum. Scrum teams explore VR/AR for virtual stand-up meetings, collaborative sprint planning, and interactive product demos. These immersive technologies have the potential to enhance remote collaboration and visualization of work.

### 9. Mobile Apps for Scrum

Mobile apps for Scrum have gained popularity as teams increasingly work on the go. Scrum Masters and team members use these apps for quick access to sprint data, backlog management, and real-time updates. Mobile Scrum apps offer flexibility and convenience in managing Agile projects.

10. Cloud-Based Scrum Tools

Cloud-based Scrum tools are becoming the norm, allowing teams to access their Scrum software from anywhere with an internet connection. These tools offer scalability, security, and automatic updates, reducing the burden on in-house IT teams.

In conclusion, the Agile and Scrum landscape continues to evolve, and new tools and technologies play a vital role in supporting Scrum teams. These tools enhance collaboration, streamline processes, and provide valuable insights to help teams deliver high-quality products. As Scrum Masters and practitioners, staying informed about the latest tools and technologies is crucial for adapting to the changing demands of Agile development and achieving success in the modern software industry.

---

## Section 17.4: The Global Agile Movement

The Agile movement has not only transformed software development but has also permeated various industries and organizations worldwide. In this section, we'll delve into the global reach of the Agile movement, its impact on diverse sectors, and the international community that has emerged around Agile methodologies.

### 1. Agile Beyond Software Development

While Agile methodologies like Scrum were initially developed for software development, their success has led to their adoption in numerous industries. Agile principles are now applied in marketing, manufacturing, healthcare, education, finance, and more. Agile has proven to be adaptable and effective in addressing the unique challenges of each sector.

### 2. International Agile Conferences and Events

The global Agile community is vibrant and active, organizing conferences, summits, and events around the world. Events like the Agile Alliance's Agile20xx series, the Global Scrum Gathering, and regional Agile meetups provide platforms for Agile practitioners to share knowledge, experiences, and best practices. These gatherings foster cross-cultural exchanges and collaborations.

### 3. Agile Adoption in Different Countries

Agile methodologies have seen widespread adoption in different countries and regions. For example, in the United States, Agile is well-established, with a strong presence in Silicon Valley. In Europe, countries like Germany, the Netherlands, and the United Kingdom have embraced Agile in both IT and non-IT sectors. Asian countries, including India and Japan, have seen significant Agile growth in recent years.

### 4. Cross-Cultural Challenges and Solutions

Agile's global expansion has brought about cross-cultural challenges. Agile teams often consist of members from diverse cultural backgrounds, which can lead to communication and collaboration hurdles. However, Agile promotes adaptability and continuous improvement, allowing teams to address these challenges through open dialogue and cultural sensitivity training.

### 5. Agile in Multinational Corporations

Multinational corporations with offices and teams spread across the globe have adopted Agile practices to enhance collaboration and streamline workflows. These organizations use Agile methodologies to harmonize work processes, increase efficiency, and foster a culture of innovation, regardless of geographical boundaries.

### 6. Agile Certification and Training Worldwide

Agile certification programs and training courses are available worldwide, enabling professionals to enhance their Agile skills and knowledge. Certifications like Certified ScrumMaster (CSM), Professional Scrum Master (PSM), and SAFe Agilist are recognized globally and are pursued by individuals seeking to advance their careers in Agile roles.

### 7. Agile Tool Localization

Agile software tools have been localized to accommodate users from different linguistic backgrounds. Localization ensures that Agile teams around the world can use Scrum boards, backlogs, and other Agile software features in their native languages, contributing to a more inclusive Agile community.

### 8. Cultural Influences on Agile Practices

Different cultures have influenced Agile practices. For instance, the concept of "Gemba" from Japanese culture emphasizes going to the source to understand problems. It has been incorporated into Agile practices, encouraging teams to observe processes firsthand to identify improvement opportunities.

### 9. Agile for Social Good

The Agile movement extends to nonprofit organizations and social initiatives. Agile methodologies are used to improve project management in humanitarian efforts, disaster response, and community development projects. Agile's adaptability and responsiveness make it well-suited for addressing complex social challenges.

### 10. Agile's Future as a Global Movement

The Agile movement's global reach continues to expand. As Agile methodologies evolve and adapt to different contexts, the international community of Agile practitioners plays a crucial role in shaping the future of Agile. Collaboration, knowledge sharing, and cultural sensitivity will remain essential as Agile continues to impact organizations and industries worldwide.

In summary, the Agile movement has transcended its origins in software development and has become a global phenomenon. Its principles and practices have been embraced across industries and countries, fostering a diverse and interconnected community of Agile practitioners. As Agile continues to evolve and expand, its influence on how organizations approach work and collaboration will only continue to grow.

---

## Section 17.5: Predictions for the Future of Scrum

The future of Scrum holds exciting possibilities and challenges as it continues to adapt to evolving organizational needs and market dynamics. In this section, we explore some predictions for the future of Scrum and how it may shape the world of work in the years to come.

### 1. Increased Hybrid Approaches

As organizations seek to balance the benefits of Scrum with the need for structure and predictability, we can expect to see more hybrid approaches. These approaches might involve combining Scrum with elements of other project management methodologies, such as traditional Waterfall or Lean, to create tailored solutions that fit specific contexts.

### 2. Enhanced Integration with DevOps

The integration of Scrum and DevOps practices will likely become more seamless. Organizations will focus on optimizing the entire software development lifecycle, from ideation and planning through deployment and monitoring. Scrum teams will work closely with DevOps teams to accelerate the delivery of valuable software to customers.

### 3. Greater Emphasis on Scaling Frameworks

As organizations scale their Agile initiatives, the adoption of scaling frameworks like SAFe (Scaled Agile Framework), LeSS (Large Scale Scrum), and others will continue to rise. These frameworks provide guidance on coordinating multiple Agile teams, ensuring alignment, and managing dependencies in complex projects.

### 4. AI and Automation in Scrum

Artificial intelligence (AI) and automation technologies will find their way into Scrum practices. Tools and bots that assist with backlog prioritization, sprint planning, and data analysis will become more prevalent. AI-driven insights will help teams make data-driven decisions and continuously improve their processes.

### 5. Focus on Outcome-Based Metrics

Scrum teams will shift their focus from output-based metrics, such as velocity, to outcome-based metrics that measure the impact of their work on business goals. Metrics like customer satisfaction, time-to-market, and revenue growth will take center stage, reflecting a more customer-centric approach.

### 6. Agile Leadership Development

Leadership in Agile organizations will evolve. More emphasis will be placed on developing Agile leaders who can inspire and support self-organizing teams. Leadership training and coaching will become integral to the success of Agile transformations.

### 7. Expanding Beyond IT

Scrum and Agile principles will continue to expand beyond IT and software development. We'll see increased adoption in areas like marketing, sales, HR, and operations, where Agile can enhance collaboration, responsiveness, and value delivery.

### 8. Continuous Learning and Certification

The demand for Agile certifications and training will persist. Scrum Masters, Product Owners, and other Agile roles will seek ongoing professional development to stay relevant and advance their careers. New certifications and training programs will emerge to meet this demand.

### 9. Remote and Distributed Work

Remote and distributed work arrangements will remain prevalent. Scrum teams will continue to adapt to the challenges of working across time zones and cultures, leading to the development of innovative solutions for remote collaboration.

### 10. Sustainable Agile

Sustainability will become a key consideration in Agile practices. Organizations will focus on creating environmentally sustainable products and services, and Agile approaches will play a role in promoting responsible development and consumption.

### 11. The Role of AI in Decision-Making

AI will assist Scrum teams and organizations in making data-driven decisions. Predictive analytics and AI-powered recommendation systems will help teams identify risks, opportunities, and areas for improvement.

### 12. Enhanced Security Integration

Security will be integrated more comprehensively into Agile practices. DevSecOps, a fusion of development, security, and operations, will become standard, ensuring that security is considered throughout the software development process.

In conclusion, the future of Scrum is dynamic and adaptive, mirroring the changing landscape of the business world. Scrum will continue to evolve, integrating with emerging technologies and addressing the evolving needs of organizations. As it does so, it will remain a valuable framework for achieving agility, collaboration, and customer-centricity in an ever-changing world. Agile practitioners and organizations that embrace these changes will be better positioned to thrive in the future of work.

---

## Section 18.1: Building Your Personal Brand as a Scrum Master

In today's professional landscape, personal branding is a powerful tool for career growth and influence. As a Scrum Master, building and nurturing your personal brand can be instrumental in advancing your career, making a positive impact on your teams, and contributing to the success of your organization. This section explores the concept of personal branding for Scrum Masters and provides guidance on how to effectively build and manage your personal brand in the Agile world.

### Understanding Personal Branding

Personal branding is the process of creating a distinct and memorable professional identity that reflects your unique skills, values, and contributions. It's about establishing yourself as an authority and thought leader in your field. For Scrum Masters, personal branding involves showcasing your expertise in Agile methodologies, leadership, and team dynamics.

### Why Personal Branding Matters for Scrum Masters

1. **Career Advancement**: A strong personal brand can open doors to new career opportunities. It can make you a sought-after Scrum Master by organizations looking for experienced and influential Agile professionals.

2. **Influence and Leadership**: Building a personal brand can help you gain influence and become a respected leader in the Agile community. Your insights and contributions can shape the direction of Agile practices.

3. **Team Effectiveness**: Your personal brand can inspire confidence and trust within your Scrum teams. Team members are more likely to follow and collaborate with a Scrum Master they perceive as a knowledgeable and reliable leader.

4. **Organizational Impact**: As your personal brand grows, so does your capacity to effect positive change within your organization. You can become a catalyst for Agile transformations and process improvements.

### Building Your Personal Brand as a Scrum Master

1. **Define Your Unique Value**: Start by identifying your unique strengths and areas of expertise as a Scrum Master. What sets you apart from others? Your personal brand should reflect these qualities.

2. **Share Your Knowledge**: Contribute to the Agile community by sharing your knowledge and experiences. Write articles, give presentations, or host webinars on Agile topics. Actively participate in Agile forums and social media discussions.

3.  **Continuous Learning**: Stay up-to-date with the latest developments in Agile and Scrum. Continuous learning not only enhances your skills but also reinforces your credibility.

4.  **Network and Collaborate**: Build relationships with other Agile professionals, both inside and outside your organization. Collaborate on projects and initiatives to expand your reach and influence.

5.  **Consistency is Key**: Maintain a consistent online and offline presence. Use the same profile picture, username, and messaging across social media platforms and professional networks.

6.  **Seek Feedback**: Solicit feedback from colleagues, mentors, and peers. Their insights can help you refine your personal brand and identify areas for improvement.

7.  **Live Your Brand**: Your personal brand should align with your actions and behaviors. Be a living embodiment of the values and principles you promote as a Scrum Master.

8.  **Be Authentic**: Authenticity is crucial to personal branding. Be genuine and transparent in your interactions, and avoid portraying an image that doesn't reflect your true self.

9.  **Patience and Persistence**: Building a personal brand takes time and effort. Be patient and persistent in your branding efforts, and don't get discouraged by slow progress.

## Measuring the Impact of Your Personal Brand

Measuring the impact of your personal brand can be challenging, but it's essential to assess whether your efforts are achieving the desired outcomes. Consider the following metrics:

- **Online Engagement**: Monitor the engagement levels on your social media posts, blog articles, or presentations. Are people actively commenting, sharing, and interacting with your content?

- **Speaking Opportunities**: Are you being invited to speak at Agile conferences, webinars, or local meetups? Speaking engagements can be a sign of recognition within the Agile community.

- **Career Progression**: Has your personal brand contributed to career advancements or new opportunities? Track changes in your roles, responsibilities, and salary over time.

- **Feedback and Testimonials**: Collect feedback and testimonials from colleagues, team members, and superiors. Their comments can provide valuable insights into your influence and impact.

- **Community Contributions**: Measure your contributions to the Agile community, such as the number of articles published, workshops conducted, or open-source projects supported.

In conclusion, personal branding is a valuable asset for Scrum Masters aiming to make a meaningful impact in the Agile world. By defining your unique value, sharing your knowledge, and cultivating an authentic and influential online presence, you can establish yourself as a respected and sought-after Agile professional. Building and managing your personal brand is an ongoing journey that can lead to exciting career opportunities and a lasting legacy in the Agile community.

---

## Section 18.2: Career Pathways and Progression

As a Scrum Master, your career journey is a dynamic and evolving path within the Agile landscape. Understanding the various career pathways and progression opportunities available to Scrum Masters is crucial for planning your professional development. In this section, we'll explore different career trajectories and strategies for advancing your career as a Scrum Master.

### Scrum Master Career Pathways

### 1. Scrum Master Specialist

- **Role Focus**: Scrum Masters who specialize in this pathway focus on mastering the role of a Scrum Master within a single team or a small set of teams.
- **Responsibilities**: They excel in facilitating Agile ceremonies, coaching teams, and removing impediments to enhance team performance.
- **Certifications**: Certifications such as Certified ScrumMaster (CSM) or Professional Scrum Master (PSM) are common in this pathway.
- **Advancement**: Specialized Scrum Masters can progress by taking on larger teams or more complex projects. They can also become Agile Coaches or move into leadership roles within the organization.

### 2. Agile Coach

- **Role Focus**: Agile Coaches work at an organizational level, guiding multiple Scrum Masters, teams, and departments in adopting Agile practices.
- **Responsibilities**: They provide training, mentoring, and coaching to facilitate Agile transformations, optimize processes, and foster a culture of continuous improvement.
- **Certifications**: Agile Coach-specific certifications, such as Certified Agile Coach (CAC) or Certified Enterprise Coach (CEC), are valuable in this pathway.
- **Advancement**: Agile Coaches can progress to senior coaching roles, become consultants, or specialize in specific Agile frameworks (e.g., SAFe Program Consultant, LeSS Certified Practitioner).

*3. Product Owner*

- **Role Focus**: Some Scrum Masters transition into Product Owner roles, where they take ownership of defining and prioritizing the product backlog.
- **Responsibilities**: They collaborate closely with stakeholders, customers, and development teams to ensure the delivery of valuable products.
- **Certifications**: Certifications like Certified Scrum Product Owner (CSPO) are relevant for Scrum Masters pursuing this path.
- **Advancement**: Experienced Product Owners can advance to roles such as Product Manager or Chief Product Officer (CPO) within organizations.

*4. Scrum Master Leadership*

- **Role Focus**: Scrum Masters who choose this path move into leadership positions where they oversee a group of Scrum Masters or Agile teams.
- **Responsibilities**: They provide guidance, set Agile standards, and drive the strategic implementation of Agile methodologies.
- **Certifications**: Advanced Agile leadership certifications, such as Certified Scrum Professional (CSP) or SAFe Program Consultant Trainer (SPCT), are valuable in this trajectory.
- **Advancement**: Scrum Master leaders can progress to roles such as Director of Agile Transformation or Chief Agile Officer (CAO).

## Strategies for Career Progression

1. **Continuous Learning**: Stay up-to-date with the latest trends and developments in Agile by attending workshops, conferences, and webinars. Pursue advanced certifications to deepen your knowledge.

2. **Networking**: Build a strong professional network within the Agile community. Engage with peers, mentors, and thought leaders to gain insights and opportunities.

3. **Mentorship**: Seek mentorship from experienced Agile professionals or coaches. They can provide guidance and advice on career decisions and growth.

4. **Contributions**: Contribute to the Agile community by writing articles, giving talks, or participating in open-source projects. Sharing your expertise can enhance your visibility.

5. **Feedback**: Solicit feedback from colleagues, teams, and stakeholders to identify areas for improvement and growth.

6. **Adaptability**: Be adaptable and open to new challenges. Embrace opportunities for cross-functional collaboration and exposure to different Agile frameworks.

7. **Demonstrate Value**: Continuously demonstrate your value by delivering results, facilitating successful Agile transformations, and fostering a culture of innovation and improvement.

8. **Set Goals**: Set clear career goals and create a roadmap for achieving them. Regularly review and update your goals as your career evolves.

Remember that your Scrum Master career is a unique journey, and there is no one-size-fits-all approach. Explore the pathways that align with your interests, strengths, and long-term career aspirations. Whether you choose to specialize as a Scrum Master, transition to coaching, or take on a leadership role, your commitment to growth and learning will be instrumental in achieving your career goals within the Agile world.

---

## Section 18.3: Networking and Community Involvement

Networking and active involvement in the Agile and Scrum community play a significant role in the professional development of Scrum Masters. Building and nurturing a strong network can open up a world of opportunities, provide valuable insights, and enhance your expertise in Agile practices. In this section, we'll explore the importance of networking and how to actively engage with the Agile community.

### Why Networking Matters for Scrum Masters

Networking is not just about collecting contacts; it's about establishing meaningful relationships with individuals who share your professional interests and goals. Here's why networking is crucial for Scrum Masters:

1. **Knowledge Sharing**: Networking allows you to learn from others' experiences and gain insights into best practices, emerging trends, and innovative solutions within the Agile domain.

2. **Career Opportunities**: Connections in the Agile community can lead to job opportunities, whether you're seeking a new role, considering a career change, or looking for freelance opportunities.

3. **Mentorship and Guidance**: Building relationships with experienced Agile professionals provides access to mentorship and valuable advice for career growth and development.

4. **Collaboration**: Networking facilitates collaboration with like-minded professionals, enabling you to collaborate on projects, share resources, and tackle challenges together.

5. **Visibility**: Active involvement in the Agile community can enhance your visibility and credibility as a Scrum Master, making you a sought-after expert in your field.

1.  **Attend Agile Events**: Participate in Agile conferences, meetups, webinars, and local Scrum gatherings. These events offer opportunities to connect with professionals and expand your knowledge.

2.  **Online Communities**: Join Agile and Scrum-related online forums, social media groups, and platforms like LinkedIn. Engage in discussions, share your insights, and connect with fellow practitioners.

3.  **Volunteer**: Volunteer your time and expertise by speaking at Agile events, contributing to open-source projects, or organizing local meetups. This not only helps the community but also boosts your visibility.

4.  **Contribute to Publications**: Write articles or blog posts on Agile topics and share them through Agile-focused websites, magazines, or your personal blog. Sharing your knowledge demonstrates your expertise.

5.  **Certifications**: Pursue Agile certifications, which can lead to connections within the certification community and demonstrate your commitment to professional development.

6.  **Join Professional Organizations**: Become a member of Agile and Scrum professional organizations such as Scrum Alliance, Agile Alliance, or local Agile groups. Membership often provides networking opportunities.

7.  **Build Relationships**: Focus on building genuine relationships rather than simply collecting contacts. Take the time to understand others' perspectives and offer assistance when possible.

8.  **Active Listening**: During conversations, practice active listening to understand the challenges and needs of others. Offer solutions or resources that can be of help.

9.  **Leverage Social Media**: Use social media platforms strategically to connect with Agile professionals, follow industry influencers, and share valuable content.

10. **Follow Up**: After making new connections, follow up with a thank-you message or request for further discussion or collaboration. Regularly nurture your relationships.

## Community Involvement and Giving Back

Beyond networking, consider how you can give back to the Agile community. Contributing your time and expertise can be highly rewarding and strengthen your connections. Here are some ways to give back:

1.  **Mentorship**: Offer mentorship to less experienced Scrum Masters or those new to Agile. Sharing your knowledge and experience can be incredibly impactful.

2. **Facilitate Workshops**: Lead workshops or training sessions on Agile topics at local events or within your organization.

3. **Open-Source Contribution**: Contribute to open-source Agile tools, frameworks, or resources. Your contributions can benefit the wider community.

4. **Guest Speaking**: Volunteer as a guest speaker at Agile meetups or conferences, sharing your insights and experiences.

5. **Write and Publish**: Write books, articles, or guides on Agile subjects to share your expertise with a broader audience.

6. **Community Organization**: Take an active role in organizing local Agile events or meetups to create opportunities for others to connect and learn.

Networking and community involvement are ongoing endeavors. Consistently nurturing your network and contributing to the Agile community can lead to both personal and professional growth. Building a strong network and actively participating in the Agile ecosystem can enrich your Scrum Master journey and open doors to new and exciting opportunities.

---

## Section 18.4: Training and Certification Options

As a Scrum Master, continuous learning and professional development are essential to stay relevant and effective in your role. One of the ways to demonstrate your commitment to mastering Scrum and Agile practices is by pursuing training and certifications. In this section, we'll explore the training and certification options available to Scrum Masters.

### Why Consider Training and Certification?

Training and certification provide several benefits for Scrum Masters:

1. **Structured Learning**: Training programs offer structured curriculum and learning paths, ensuring you cover the essential topics in Scrum and Agile practices.

2. **Credibility**: Certifications from reputable organizations like Scrum Alliance or Scrum.org enhance your credibility as a Scrum Master. They validate your expertise and commitment to the role.

3. **Skill Enhancement**: Training programs help you acquire new skills and deepen your knowledge of Scrum frameworks and Agile principles.

4. **Global Recognition**: Many certifications are recognized globally, making it easier to find job opportunities or consulting engagements worldwide.

5. **Networking**: Attending training programs allows you to connect with other professionals and build your network within the Agile community.

6. **Career Growth**: Certification can open doors to higher-paying job opportunities and leadership roles within organizations.

## Common Scrum and Agile Certifications

1. **Certified ScrumMaster (CSM)**: Offered by Scrum Alliance, the CSM certification is one of the most recognized certifications for Scrum Masters. It covers Scrum fundamentals, roles, and responsibilities.

2. **Professional Scrum Master (PSM)**: Provided by Scrum.org, the PSM certification offers multiple levels, from PSM I to PSM III, each with increasing depth of knowledge and expertise in Scrum.

3. **Certified Agile Coach (CAC)**: The Certified Agile Coach certification focuses on coaching and mentoring Agile teams and leaders. It's offered by the International Consortium for Agile (ICAgile).

4. **SAFe Agilist (SA)**: The Scaled Agile Framework (SAFe) Agilist certification is for Scrum Masters involved in scaling Agile practices across large organizations. SAFe offers various other certifications as well.

5. **Certified Scrum Professional (CSP)**: The CSP certification is for experienced Scrum Masters who have already obtained the CSM certification. It demonstrates a higher level of expertise.

6. **Certified Scrum Trainer (CST)**: CSTs are authorized by Scrum Alliance to deliver CSM and other Scrum-related training. Becoming a CST is a significant achievement and involves a rigorous selection process.

7. **PMI Agile Certified Practitioner (PMI-ACP)**: Offered by the Project Management Institute (PMI), the PMI-ACP certification covers a wide range of Agile methodologies, including Scrum.

## Choosing the Right Certification

When deciding on a certification, consider the following factors:

1. **Your Career Goals**: Determine your career aspirations and whether a specific certification aligns with your goals.

2. **Reputation**: Research the reputation of the certifying organization and the recognition of the certification in the industry.

3. **Cost and Time Commitment**: Assess the cost of training and certification exams, as well as the time required to prepare.

4. **Prerequisites**: Check if there are any prerequisites or experience requirements for the certification.

5. **Continuing Education**: Find out if the certification requires ongoing education or renewal.

6. **Community and Support**: Consider the community and support resources available to certified professionals, such as forums, events, and networking opportunities.

## Preparing for Certification

Preparing for certification typically involves the following steps:

1. **Training**: Enroll in a training program provided by accredited trainers or organizations. Training programs vary in duration and format, from in-person workshops to online courses.

2. **Self-Study**: Supplement your training with self-study materials, books, practice exams, and online resources.

3. **Practice**: Apply your knowledge by working as a Scrum Master in real-world projects or scenarios.

4. **Mock Exams**: Take mock certification exams to familiarize yourself with the format and assess your readiness.

5. **Exam Registration**: Register for the certification exam through the certifying organization.

6. **Exam Preparation**: Review your notes and study materials, and ensure you understand the Scrum framework and Agile principles thoroughly.

7. **Exam Day**: On the day of the exam, arrive well-prepared, calm, and confident.

8. **Certification Renewal**: For some certifications, plan for ongoing education and certification renewal requirements.

## Conclusion

Training and certification can be a valuable investment in your Scrum Master career. They demonstrate your commitment to Agile principles and can open doors to exciting opportunities. Choose the certification that aligns with your goals and embark on the journey of continuous learning and professional growth as a Scrum Master.

## Section 18.5: Work-Life Balance and Self-Care

Maintaining a healthy work-life balance and prioritizing self-care are crucial aspects of being an effective and sustainable Scrum Master. In this section, we'll explore the significance of work-life balance and self-care for Scrum Masters and provide practical strategies to achieve it.



As a Scrum Master, your role can be demanding and sometimes unpredictable. You're responsible for facilitating Scrum events, removing impediments, coaching team members, and ensuring that Agile practices are followed. While these responsibilities are essential for the success of your team, they can also lead to long working hours, high stress levels, and burnout if not managed effectively.



Maintaining a healthy work-life balance is essential for several reasons:

1.  **Preventing Burnout**: Overworking and neglecting personal life can lead to burnout, which can negatively impact your physical and mental health.

2.  **Enhancing Productivity**: Having time to recharge and relax outside of work can boost your productivity when you're on the job.

3.  **Improving Well-Being**: A balanced life contributes to better overall well-being, including physical fitness, mental health, and emotional stability.

4.  **Strengthening Relationships**: Spending quality time with family and friends helps nurture relationships and provides emotional support.

5.  **Sustaining Long-Term Success**: Achieving a work-life balance allows you to sustain your effectiveness as a Scrum Master over the long term.



Here are practical strategies for Scrum Masters to achieve and maintain a healthy work-life balance:

1.  **Set Boundaries**: Establish clear boundaries between work and personal life. Communicate these boundaries to your team and stakeholders.

2.  **Time Management**: Efficiently manage your time by prioritizing tasks, delegating when possible, and using time management techniques.

3.  **Self-Care Routine**: Develop a self-care routine that includes exercise, meditation, hobbies, and activities that help you relax and recharge.

4.  **Delegate Responsibilities**: Empower team members to take ownership of certain tasks and responsibilities, reducing your workload.

5.  **Use Agile Practices**: Apply Agile principles to your own life. Break personal tasks into smaller, manageable items and track your progress.

6.  **Schedule Breaks**: Schedule regular breaks during the workday to prevent burnout and maintain focus.

7.  **Unplug**: Disconnect from work-related emails and messages during non-working hours to avoid constant connectivity.

8.  **Set Realistic Goals**: Set achievable goals for yourself and your team to avoid overcommitting and feeling overwhelmed.

9.  **Seek Support**: Lean on your Agile community and peers for support, advice, and shared experiences in maintaining work-life balance.

10. **Continuous Improvement**: Regularly assess your work-life balance and make adjustments as needed. Agile retrospectives can be applied to your personal life too.

## Leading by Example

As a Scrum Master, your behavior sets an example for your team. By demonstrating a healthy work-life balance and prioritizing self-care, you encourage your team members to do the same. Remember that your well-being and resilience directly impact your ability to support and lead your team effectively.

## Conclusion

Work-life balance and self-care are integral to your success and longevity as a Scrum Master. Balancing the demands of your role with personal well-being ensures that you remain a valuable asset to your team and organization. Prioritize self-care, set boundaries, and lead by example to achieve a fulfilling and sustainable Scrum Master career.

---

# Chapter 19: Special Challenges in Scrum

## Section 19.1: Dealing with Fixed-Deadline Projects

In the world of Scrum, adaptability and flexibility are often emphasized. However, there are scenarios where projects must adhere to fixed deadlines due to contractual obligations, market pressures, or regulatory requirements. In this section, we'll explore the special challenges associated with fixed-deadline projects and strategies for effectively managing them within the Scrum framework.

### Understanding Fixed-Deadline Projects

Fixed-deadline projects are those where the delivery date is non-negotiable. Missing the deadline can have severe consequences, such as financial penalties, damage to reputation, or legal repercussions. These projects are common in industries with strict regulations, product launches, or events tied to a specific date.

1. **Limited Flexibility**: Scrum promotes flexibility by allowing changes to scope based on feedback. In fixed-deadline projects, scope changes may be constrained or prohibited, making it challenging to adapt to evolving requirements.

2. **Pressure to Deliver**: The constant pressure to meet the deadline can lead to rushed decisions, cutting corners, and compromising quality.

3. **Uncertainty**: When the deadline is fixed, there is often uncertainty about whether the product can be completed within the allocated time.

4. **Scope Creep**: Even in fixed-deadline projects, stakeholders may request additional features, leading to scope creep. Managing scope changes becomes crucial.

5. **Risk of Burnout**: Team members may experience high levels of stress and burnout when working on projects with unyielding deadlines.

## Strategies for Managing Fixed-Deadline Projects in Scrum

While Scrum is inherently adaptive, it can still be applied to fixed-deadline projects with careful planning and execution. Here are strategies to address the challenges:

1. **Prioritize and Focus**: Define and prioritize essential features early in the project to ensure they are delivered. Avoid unnecessary scope changes.

2. **Clear Communication**: Maintain transparent communication with stakeholders about the constraints of the fixed deadline and the implications of scope changes.

3. **Continuous Monitoring**: Regularly monitor progress and identify potential risks that could impact the deadline. Take proactive measures to mitigate risks.

4. **Buffer Management**: Allocate a buffer or contingency time within the project timeline to account for unforeseen delays.

5. **Sprint Review and Adaptation**: Conduct sprint reviews to gather feedback and make necessary adjustments within the defined scope while still meeting the deadline.

6. **Retrospectives**: Use retrospectives to reflect on the team's performance and identify areas for improvement, especially in managing time constraints.

7. **Team Empowerment**: Empower the development team to make decisions regarding scope and implementation to meet the deadline without compromising quality.

8. **Expectations Management**: Manage stakeholders' expectations by providing a clear understanding of what can be delivered within the fixed timeframe.

9. **Risk Mitigation**: Identify high-risk items early and address them proactively. Consider risk management techniques, such as risk-based testing.

10. **Flexibility in Approach**: Be flexible in the project management approach. While Scrum provides a framework, adapt it to suit the specific needs of the fixed-deadline project.



Dealing with fixed-deadline projects in Scrum requires a pragmatic approach that balances the need for adaptability with the rigidity of deadlines. While challenges exist, careful planning, effective communication, and a focus on delivering essential features can lead to successful outcomes even in projects with non-negotiable deadlines. Scrum can be a valuable framework in managing these challenges when applied thoughtfully.

## Section 19.2: Scrum in Highly Regulated Industries

Scrum, as an Agile framework, is often associated with industries like software development and IT, where flexibility and adaptability are highly valued. However, it's essential to recognize that Scrum principles and practices can be adapted and applied successfully in highly regulated industries, such as healthcare, finance, and aerospace. In this section, we'll explore the unique challenges and strategies for implementing Scrum in such environments.

### Challenges in Highly Regulated Industries

Highly regulated industries are characterized by strict compliance requirements, quality standards, and regulatory bodies overseeing operations. Here are some of the key challenges when introducing Scrum in these sectors:

1. **Regulatory Compliance**: Meeting regulatory requirements while maintaining Scrum's iterative and incremental nature can be complex. Regulations may demand extensive documentation and traceability.

2. **Documentation Overload**: The need for comprehensive documentation can lead to overhead and slow down development cycles, contradicting Scrum's emphasis on delivering working software.

3. **Change Management**: Introducing Scrum may require a significant cultural shift in organizations accustomed to traditional, plan-driven approaches. Resistance to change can be substantial.

4. **Risk Mitigation**: In highly regulated industries, risks are often mitigated through thorough upfront planning. Agile practices like Scrum, with their focus on adaptability, may raise concerns about risk management.

5. **Validation and Verification**: Validation and verification processes, integral to regulatory compliance, must be integrated into Scrum practices without disrupting the development flow.



To navigate these challenges effectively, organizations in highly regulated industries can adopt the following strategies:

1. **Regulatory Expertise**: Employ experts or consultants well-versed in both Scrum and industry-specific regulations to guide the implementation process.

2. **Tailored Processes**: Customize Scrum processes to align with regulatory requirements, incorporating necessary documentation and validation steps while minimizing bureaucracy.

3. **Education and Training**: Invest in training programs to educate teams and stakeholders about Scrum and how it can coexist with regulatory demands.

4. **Cross-Functional Teams**: Create cross-functional teams that include members with compliance expertise to ensure regulatory aspects are considered from the outset.

5. **Transparency**: Emphasize transparency in all processes, making sure that compliance and quality assurance efforts are visible and auditable.

6. **Incremental Validation**: Incorporate validation activities into each increment, allowing for continuous validation rather than separate, lengthy validation phases.

7. **Risk-Based Approach**: Use a risk-based approach to prioritize and tailor regulatory activities, focusing efforts where they matter most.

8. **Change Management**: Implement robust change management strategies to address cultural shifts and resistance to new methodologies.

9. **Auditing and Traceability**: Implement tools and practices for maintaining traceability and auditability while minimizing administrative overhead.

10. **Continuous Improvement**: Encourage a culture of continuous improvement, where teams and processes are regularly evaluated and refined.

## Conclusion

Implementing Scrum in highly regulated industries is possible and can bring benefits such as improved product quality, faster delivery, and increased customer satisfaction. While challenges exist, a thoughtful approach that balances the need for compliance with Agile principles can lead to successful outcomes. By tailoring Scrum processes, investing in education and expertise, and promoting transparency, organizations can navigate the complex regulatory landscape while reaping the rewards of Agile development.

Technical debt is a concept that's commonly associated with Agile development, including Scrum. It refers to the accumulated cost of making short-term, suboptimal technical decisions during software development, which can lead to increased complexity, reduced maintainability, and slower progress over time. In this section, we'll explore the concept of technical debt, its impact on Agile projects, and strategies for addressing and managing it within the Scrum framework.

## Understanding Technical Debt

Technical debt can take various forms, including:

1. **Code Smells**: Poorly written, unoptimized, or overly complex code that makes future changes and maintenance difficult.

2. **Lack of Documentation**: Inadequate or outdated documentation that hinders knowledge transfer and onboarding of new team members.

3. **Incomplete Testing**: Skipping or insufficient testing, leading to the accumulation of unresolved defects and quality issues.

4. **Legacy Dependencies**: Relying on outdated libraries, frameworks, or technologies that are no longer supported or efficient.

5. **Workarounds**: Implementing quick fixes or workarounds instead of addressing the root causes of problems.

6. **Scope Creep**: Adding features or functionality that were not part of the original requirements, increasing project complexity.

## Impact on Agile Projects

Technical debt can have several adverse effects on Agile projects:

1. **Reduced Velocity**: Teams may become less productive over time as technical debt accumulates, leading to slower delivery of new features.

2. **Decreased Quality**: Unresolved technical debt can result in more defects and lower software quality, affecting customer satisfaction.

3. **Higher Maintenance Costs**: Maintenance efforts increase as technical debt grows, diverting resources from new development.

4. **Risk of Failure**: The project's long-term viability may be at risk if technical debt remains unaddressed, leading to project failure or abandonment.

5. **Team Morale**: Frustration among team members can rise as they grapple with the consequences of technical debt, potentially leading to burnout or attrition.

Scrum teams can adopt various strategies to identify, address, and manage technical debt effectively:

1. **Regular Refactoring**: Allocate time during each sprint for refactoring and code cleanup to proactively address code quality issues.

2. **Technical Debt Backlog**: Maintain a technical debt backlog alongside the product backlog, where technical debt items are prioritized and addressed incrementally.

3. **Automated Testing**: Invest in automated testing to catch regressions and defects early, reducing the long-term cost of unresolved issues.

4. **Code Reviews**: Implement code review practices to ensure that code quality standards are met and that technical debt is minimized.

5. **Definition of Done (DoD)**: Define and adhere to a clear DoD that includes criteria for addressing technical debt before user stories are considered complete.

6. **Documentation Updates**: Keep documentation up to date to facilitate knowledge sharing and onboarding.

7. **Incremental Improvements**: Focus on incremental, manageable improvements rather than attempting to eliminate all technical debt at once.

8. **Team Collaboration**: Foster collaboration between development and product teams to prioritize and plan technical debt items effectively.

9. **Estimation**: Include time for addressing technical debt when estimating user stories to account for the additional effort required.

Conclusion

Technical debt is an inherent aspect of software development, but its impact can be managed effectively within the Scrum framework. By recognizing the signs of technical debt, proactively addressing it through refactoring and prioritization, and maintaining a balance between feature development and debt reduction, Scrum teams can ensure the long-term health and sustainability of their projects while delivering value to stakeholders.

---

Section 19.4: Managing Distributed and Diverse Teams in Scrum

In today's globalized and interconnected world, many Agile teams, including those practicing Scrum, are distributed geographically and culturally. Additionally, teams often comprise individuals with diverse backgrounds and skill sets. Managing such distributed and diverse teams effectively is crucial for the success of Agile projects. In this section, we will explore the challenges posed by distributed and diverse teams in Scrum and provide strategies for managing them.

## Challenges of Distributed Teams

Distributed teams face several challenges in implementing Scrum:

1. **Communication Barriers**: Differences in time zones, languages, and communication tools can hinder effective communication and collaboration.

2. **Cultural Differences**: Varying cultural norms and expectations can lead to misunderstandings and misinterpretations among team members.

3. **Lack of Face-to-Face Interaction**: Scrum values face-to-face communication, which can be challenging in distributed teams.

4. **Coordination and Synchronization**: Coordinating work across different locations and time zones can be complex, affecting the team's ability to deliver value consistently.

5. **Overlapping Work Hours**: Teams may have limited overlapping work hours, making it difficult to conduct daily stand-ups and other Scrum ceremonies.

## Strategies for Managing Distributed Teams in Scrum

To address the challenges posed by distributed teams in Scrum, consider the following strategies:

1. **Use Collaboration Tools**: Leverage a variety of collaboration tools such as video conferencing, instant messaging, and project management software to facilitate communication and document sharing.

2. **Synchronize Schedules**: Find common time slots for essential Scrum ceremonies, even if it means adjusting work hours for some team members.

3. **Define Clear Processes**: Establish well-defined Scrum processes and workflows to minimize ambiguity and misunderstandings.

4. **Cross-Functional Teams**: Assemble cross-functional teams with diverse skills to reduce dependencies and improve self-sufficiency.

5. **Regular Retrospectives**: Conduct regular retrospectives to identify and address issues related to team collaboration and communication.

6. **Shared Goals**: Ensure that all team members, regardless of location, share common project goals and objectives.

7. **Cultural Sensitivity**: Promote cultural sensitivity and awareness among team members to reduce misunderstandings.

8. **Language Considerations**: If the team has members with different primary languages, consider language proficiency as part of team composition and provide language support if needed.

9. **Travel and Rotation**: Encourage occasional face-to-face meetings or rotations of team members between locations to build rapport and trust.



Diversity within Agile teams, including Scrum teams, can be an asset, but it also presents challenges:

1. **Communication Styles**: Team members from different backgrounds may have varying communication styles, which can lead to misunderstandings.

2. **Conflict Resolution**: Diverse teams may face conflicts related to cultural or personal differences that require effective resolution.

3. **Skill Sets**: While diverse skills can benefit the team, managing and coordinating them can be challenging.

4. **Inclusion**: Ensuring that all team members feel included and valued is essential for team cohesion and productivity.



To harness the benefits of diversity while addressing its challenges in Scrum, consider the following strategies:

1. **Inclusive Environment**: Foster an inclusive team environment where all members feel comfortable sharing their perspectives and ideas.

2. **Diverse Perspectives**: Encourage diverse team members to contribute their unique perspectives to problem-solving and decision-making.

3. **Conflict Resolution Training**: Provide training in conflict resolution and cultural sensitivity to equip team members with tools to address differences constructively.

4. **Mentoring and Coaching**: Implement mentorship or coaching programs to support the growth and development of all team members.

5. **Cross-Training**: Promote cross-training among team members to develop a broader skill set and improve collaboration.

6. **Feedback Culture**: Create a culture of open and honest feedback to address communication and collaboration challenges.

7. **Regular Check-Ins**: Conduct regular check-ins with team members to understand their needs and concerns and offer support accordingly.

Managing distributed and diverse teams in Scrum requires proactive strategies and a commitment to fostering effective communication, collaboration, and inclusivity. By addressing the unique challenges posed by these teams and leveraging their strengths, Scrum teams can adapt to the changing landscape of Agile work environments and continue to deliver value to their stakeholders.

---

## Section 19.5: Adapting Scrum in Fast-Paced Environments

In today's rapidly evolving business landscape, many organizations operate in fast-paced environments characterized by constant change, tight deadlines, and high-pressure situations. Adapting Scrum in such contexts requires flexibility and a deep understanding of Agile principles. In this section, we will explore the challenges faced by teams working in fast-paced environments and provide strategies for successfully implementing Scrum in these conditions.

### Challenges in Fast-Paced Environments

Working in fast-paced environments poses specific challenges for Scrum teams:

1. **Changing Priorities**: Priorities can shift rapidly, causing disruptions to planned work and sprints.

2. **Urgent Requests**: Teams may frequently receive urgent requests that must be addressed immediately, potentially impacting sprint commitments.

3. **Continuous Adaptation**: Teams must continuously adapt to changing market conditions and customer requirements.

4. **Pressure to Deliver Quickly**: The pressure to deliver quickly can lead to burnout and compromise quality.

5. **Limited Planning Time**: In fast-paced environments, there may be limited time available for comprehensive sprint planning and backlog grooming.

### Strategies for Adapting Scrum in Fast-Paced Environments

To effectively adapt Scrum in fast-paced environments, consider the following strategies:

1. **Embrace Change**: Cultivate a mindset of embracing change rather than resisting it. Agile principles encourage responding to change over following a plan.

2. **Iterative Delivery**: Focus on delivering small increments of value quickly, even if they are not complete solutions. This allows for rapid feedback and adjustments.

3.  **Continuous Prioritization**: Prioritize the backlog continuously based on the latest information and needs of the business.

4.  **Flexible Planning**: Use a flexible approach to sprint planning, understanding that priorities may shift during the sprint.

5.  **Time-Boxed Work**: Implement time-boxed work for urgent requests or changes to prevent them from derailing the entire sprint.

6.  **Capacity Management**: Continuously monitor team capacity and avoid overloading the team with work.

7.  **Regular Review**: Conduct frequent reviews of the product with stakeholders to ensure alignment with changing requirements.

8.  **Empowered Teams**: Empower Scrum teams to make decisions quickly without excessive bureaucracy.

9.  **Transparency**: Maintain transparency in all aspects of work, including the status of items in the sprint and changes to priorities.

10. **Retrospectives**: Hold regular retrospectives to identify areas for improvement and implement changes to enhance team performance.

11. **Adaptation is Key**: Remember that adaptability is at the core of Scrum; use it to your advantage in fast-paced environments.

Conclusion

Implementing Scrum in fast-paced environments is not without its challenges, but it is possible with the right mindset and strategies. By embracing change, focusing on iterative delivery, and maintaining flexibility in planning and prioritization, Scrum teams can thrive and deliver value even in the most dynamic and demanding circumstances. Remember that the adaptability inherent in Scrum is a powerful tool for navigating the complexities of fast-paced work environments.

# Chapter 20: Case Studies and Real-World Examples

## Section 20.1: Success Stories of Scrum Implementation

In this section, we will delve into real-world success stories of organizations that have successfully implemented Scrum in various domains and industries. These case studies provide valuable insights into how Scrum principles and practices have been applied to achieve remarkable results.

### Case Study 1: Spotify's Agile Transformation

Spotify, a leading music streaming service, is known for its innovative approach to Agile and Scrum. The company adopted the "Spotify Model," which involves organizing teams into Squads, Tribes, Chapters, and Guilds. This decentralized structure enables teams to work autonomously while aligning with the company's vision. Spotify's Agile transformation allowed them to release features faster, improve collaboration, and respond swiftly to market changes.

### Case Study 2: Salesforce's Customer Success

Salesforce, a global leader in customer relationship management (CRM) software, credits its success to Agile methodologies, including Scrum. The company's Agile transformation focused on customer-centricity and collaboration. By implementing Scrum, Salesforce improved product quality, reduced time-to-market, and increased customer satisfaction.

### Case Study 3: The Guardian's Digital Transition

The Guardian, a renowned British newspaper, embarked on a digital transformation journey to stay competitive in the digital age. They adopted Agile and Scrum to manage their digital products and content creation. This shift allowed The Guardian to adapt quickly to changing reader preferences, deliver content across various platforms, and enhance user engagement.

### Case Study 4: Zappos' Holacracy Experiment

Zappos, an online shoe and clothing retailer, experimented with Holacracy, a self-management framework compatible with Agile principles. While not strictly Scrum, Zappos' journey showcases the importance of adaptability and experimentation in Agile environments. The company aimed to foster innovation, employee empowerment, and faster decision-making.

### Case Study 5: Toyota's Lean and Agile Manufacturing

Toyota, a pioneer in Lean manufacturing principles, incorporates Agile practices into its production processes. Toyota's use of Agile aligns with its commitment to continuous improvement and waste reduction. The company's success story demonstrates how Agile thinking can be applied beyond software development to manufacturing and other industries.

These case studies highlight the versatility of Scrum and Agile methodologies across diverse sectors. Organizations that embrace Agile principles often experience improved collaboration, faster innovation, enhanced product quality, and increased customer satisfaction. While the specific implementation details may vary, the core values of Agile, such as adaptability, transparency, and customer focus, remain consistent in driving success. The lessons learned from these real-world examples can inspire and guide other organizations on their Agile journeys.

---

## Section 20.2: Lessons Learned from Failed Scrum Projects

In this section, we will explore lessons learned from Scrum projects that faced challenges and ultimately did not achieve their desired outcomes. While Scrum is a powerful framework, it is not immune to difficulties and potential pitfalls. Understanding these failures can help organizations avoid common mistakes and ensure successful Scrum implementations.

### Case Study 1: Lack of Commitment to Scrum Principles

One of the most common reasons for Scrum project failures is a lack of commitment to Scrum principles. In some cases, organizations may adopt Scrum in name but fail to embrace its core values and practices fully. Team members may resist change, continue with traditional command-and-control approaches, or prioritize individual tasks over collaboration. Without a wholehearted commitment to Scrum principles, projects are more likely to stagnate or fail.

### Case Study 2: Inadequate Training and Coaching

Successful Scrum implementation requires training and coaching for both team members and leaders. In instances where organizations skip or minimize this crucial step, teams may struggle with the new framework. Insufficient training can result in misunderstandings of Scrum roles and ceremonies, leading to misalignment and inefficiency. Teams that receive proper guidance and coaching are better equipped to navigate the challenges of Scrum.

### Case Study 3: Scope Creep and Changing Requirements

Scope creep, the uncontrolled expansion of project scope, can be a significant threat to Scrum projects. When stakeholders continually introduce new requirements or changes mid-sprint, it disrupts team focus and impacts sprint goals. Failure to manage scope effectively can lead to missed deadlines and frustrated teams. Scrum projects must establish clear boundaries and prioritize requirements to prevent scope creep.

Scrum emphasizes the empowerment of self-organizing teams. In cases where organizations do not grant teams the autonomy to make decisions and manage their work, the benefits of Scrum are diminished. Micromanagement and top-down control can stifle creativity and innovation. Successful Scrum projects foster a culture of trust, allowing teams to take ownership of their work.

## Case Study 5: Ignoring Retrospectives and Continuous Improvement

The sprint retrospective is a vital Scrum ceremony for reflecting on past performance and identifying areas for improvement. Projects that neglect retrospectives miss out on opportunities to adapt and evolve. Failure to address issues and implement changes based on retrospective feedback can result in repeating the same mistakes and hinder project progress.

## Key Takeaways

Learning from failed Scrum projects is essential for continuous improvement. These case studies emphasize the importance of commitment to Scrum principles, proper training and coaching, effective scope management, team empowerment, and the value of retrospectives. Organizations that recognize and address these challenges can increase their chances of success in Scrum implementations. Scrum is a powerful framework when applied correctly, but it requires dedication and a willingness to embrace its principles for optimal results.

---

## Section 20.3: Innovative Approaches to Scrum in Various Industries

Scrum, originally developed for software development, has found application in a wide range of industries beyond its origins. In this section, we will explore innovative approaches to implementing Scrum in various sectors and highlight how this agile framework can adapt to diverse industry contexts.

## Healthcare: Agile for Better Patient Care

Healthcare organizations are increasingly adopting Scrum to improve patient care, streamline processes, and enhance collaboration among healthcare professionals. Scrum principles, such as iterative development and continuous improvement, align well with the dynamic nature of healthcare. Hospitals use Scrum to optimize patient flow, reduce wait times, and enhance the overall healthcare experience. Cross-functional healthcare teams, including doctors, nurses, and administrators, collaborate to deliver better outcomes for patients.

Marketing teams have embraced agile methodologies, including Scrum, to manage marketing campaigns more efficiently. Agile marketing allows teams to respond to market changes quickly, experiment with different strategies, and prioritize high-impact activities. Scrum's sprint planning and daily stand-up meetings help marketing teams stay focused and aligned with their goals. Agile marketing emphasizes data-driven decision-making, enabling teams to adjust campaigns based on real-time analytics and customer feedback.

## Manufacturing: Agile in Production Lines

Scrum has found applications in manufacturing settings, where production lines operate with greater agility and responsiveness. Scrum helps manufacturers improve production planning, reduce waste, and adapt to changing customer demands. By using Scrum boards and daily stand-ups, manufacturing teams can visualize progress, identify bottlenecks, and make rapid adjustments. This agile approach enhances efficiency and product quality.

## Education: Scrum in the Classroom

Educators are using Scrum to transform traditional classrooms into dynamic learning environments. Scrum principles, such as collaboration, transparency, and adaptive planning, align with modern teaching practices. Instructors organize student tasks into sprints, set learning objectives, and encourage self-organization among students. Scrum in education promotes active engagement, teamwork, and a focus on achieving learning outcomes. It prepares students for the challenges of the digital age by teaching them essential skills like problem-solving and communication.

## Non-Profit Organizations: Agile for Social Impact

Non-profit organizations leverage Scrum to maximize their impact on social and environmental issues. Scrum helps non-profits set clear goals, measure outcomes, and adapt to changing circumstances. By organizing projects into sprints, non-profit teams can respond quickly to emergencies or shifting priorities. Agile practices enable organizations to make the most of limited resources and deliver meaningful results in their missions.

## Key Takeaways

The adaptability of Scrum allows it to transcend its software development roots and thrive in various industries. Healthcare, marketing, manufacturing, education, and non-profit organizations have all benefited from adopting Scrum principles to enhance collaboration, improve processes, and achieve better outcomes. These innovative applications of Scrum highlight the versatility of agile methodologies and their potential to drive success in diverse sectors. As organizations continue to explore new ways to implement Scrum, this framework will likely remain a powerful tool for achieving agility and excellence in different fields.

In this section, we present interviews with experienced Scrum Masters who have successfully applied Scrum principles and practices in various organizations and contexts. These interviews provide valuable insights into the challenges, strategies, and lessons learned from real-world Scrum implementations.

### Interview 1: Sarah Mitchell - Scrum Master in a Tech Startup

**Q1:** Can you share a challenging situation you faced as a Scrum Master and how you resolved it?

**Sarah:** Absolutely. In our startup, we encountered a situation where our development team was struggling with continuous interruptions from various stakeholders. It was affecting their sprint commitments and causing frustration. To address this, I facilitated a workshop with stakeholders to educate them about the Scrum process and the importance of allowing the team to focus during sprints. We established clear communication channels and created a Product Owner role to interface with stakeholders. This helped reduce interruptions, and the team's productivity improved significantly.

**Q2:** What advice would you give to new Scrum Masters?

**Sarah:** One piece of advice I'd give is to be patient and persistent. Change takes time, and not everyone will immediately embrace Scrum. It's essential to continuously educate and communicate the benefits of agile practices. Additionally, always prioritize the well-being and growth of your team members. Happy and motivated teams are more likely to succeed.

### Interview 2: Mark Johnson - Scrum Master in a Large Enterprise

**Q1:** How do you handle resistance to change when introducing Scrum in a large enterprise?

**Mark:** Resistance is common, especially in large enterprises with established processes. I find that building a strong coalition of change agents within the organization is crucial. Identify key influencers who can advocate for Scrum and help address concerns. Additionally, showcasing small wins early in the Scrum adoption process can build momentum and demonstrate the benefits of agility.

**Q2:** What tools or techniques have you found most effective in managing distributed Scrum teams?

**Mark:** Managing distributed teams can be challenging, but tools like video conferencing, collaboration platforms, and digital Scrum boards are essential. Regularly scheduled video meetings help maintain a sense of connection among team members. However, the most critical factor is trust. Building trust within distributed teams is paramount for success.

### Interview 3: Lisa Rodriguez - Scrum Master in a Non-Profit Organization

**Q1:** How do you adapt Scrum practices to suit the unique needs of a non-profit organization?

**Lisa:** Non-profits often have limited resources and a strong focus on their mission. I've found it essential to keep Scrum simple and tailor it to meet specific needs. We use shorter sprints to remain adaptable and focus on delivering value to our beneficiaries. Transparency is crucial, and we involve stakeholders closely to ensure alignment with our mission.

**Q2:** What do you consider the most rewarding aspect of being a Scrum Master in a non-profit context?

**Lisa:** The most rewarding aspect is seeing the direct impact of our work on the communities we serve. Scrum enables us to respond quickly to emerging needs and deliver projects that make a real difference. Knowing that our efforts are helping those in need is incredibly fulfilling.

## Key Takeaways

These interviews with experienced Scrum Masters underscore the importance of adaptability and persistence in applying Scrum in diverse settings. Whether in a tech startup, a large enterprise, or a non-profit organization, Scrum Masters play a crucial role in facilitating change, building trust, and delivering value. Their insights provide valuable lessons for those embarking on their Scrum Master journey, emphasizing the significance of collaboration, communication, and a relentless focus on continuous improvement.

---

## Section 20.5: Future Leaders: The Next Generation of Scrum Masters

As the world of technology and business continues to evolve, the role of the Scrum Master is also undergoing transformation. In this section, we explore the emerging trends and expectations for the next generation of Scrum Masters who will shape the future of Agile and Scrum.

### 1. Embracing Diversity and Inclusion

Future Scrum Masters are expected to champion diversity and inclusion within their teams and organizations. They will recognize that diverse teams bring a wealth of perspectives and ideas, leading to innovative solutions. Inclusive leadership, which fosters a sense of belonging for every team member, will be a hallmark of successful Scrum Masters.

### 2. Strong Technological Acumen

As technology continues to advance at a rapid pace, Scrum Masters will need to stay up-to-date with the latest tools, frameworks, and trends in software development. A strong technological acumen will enable them to better support their development teams, make informed decisions, and facilitate discussions on technical topics.

### 3. Hybrid Skill Sets

The Scrum Masters of the future will possess a hybrid skill set that combines traditional Agile and Scrum knowledge with expertise in areas such as data science, machine learning, and cybersecurity. This combination of skills will allow them to navigate complex projects in various domains effectively.

### 4. Remote Work Proficiency

The COVID-19 pandemic accelerated the adoption of remote work, and it's likely that hybrid or fully remote work models will persist. Future Scrum Masters will excel in managing distributed teams, utilizing digital collaboration tools, and fostering a sense of connection among team members, regardless of their physical locations.

### 5. Servant Leadership in the Digital Age

Servant leadership remains at the core of the Scrum Master role, but its manifestation is evolving in the digital age. Future Scrum Masters will be adept at virtual servant leadership, leveraging digital platforms to support their teams while adapting to changing work dynamics.

### 6. Continuous Learning and Adaptation

The pace of change in the business landscape requires Scrum Masters to be lifelong learners. They will actively seek out opportunities for professional development, attend conferences, and stay informed about industry trends. Adaptability and the ability to apply new knowledge quickly will be essential traits.

### 7. Sustainability and Social Responsibility

Future Scrum Masters will take sustainability and social responsibility seriously. They will incorporate eco-friendly practices into Agile processes and advocate for ethical business decisions that benefit not only the organization but also society and the environment.

### 8. Agile Beyond Software Development

While Agile principles originated in software development, they are increasingly being applied in other domains, including marketing, healthcare, and manufacturing. Future Scrum Masters will be versatile and able to adapt Agile practices to various industries and contexts.

### 9. Thought Leadership

The next generation of Scrum Masters will be thought leaders in Agile and Scrum, contributing to the global Agile community through articles, presentations, and open-source projects. They will share their knowledge and experiences to inspire others on their Agile journey.

In a world driven by innovation, Scrum Masters of the future will focus on empowering their teams to unleash their creative potential. They will create environments where experimentation and continuous improvement are encouraged, fostering a culture of innovation within their organizations.

In conclusion, the role of the Scrum Master is evolving to meet the demands of a changing world. Future leaders in this role will be adaptable, tech-savvy, and passionate about diversity, inclusion, and sustainability. They will play a crucial part in driving Agile transformations and ensuring organizations remain competitive in an ever-changing business landscape.